Contents

GW00649878

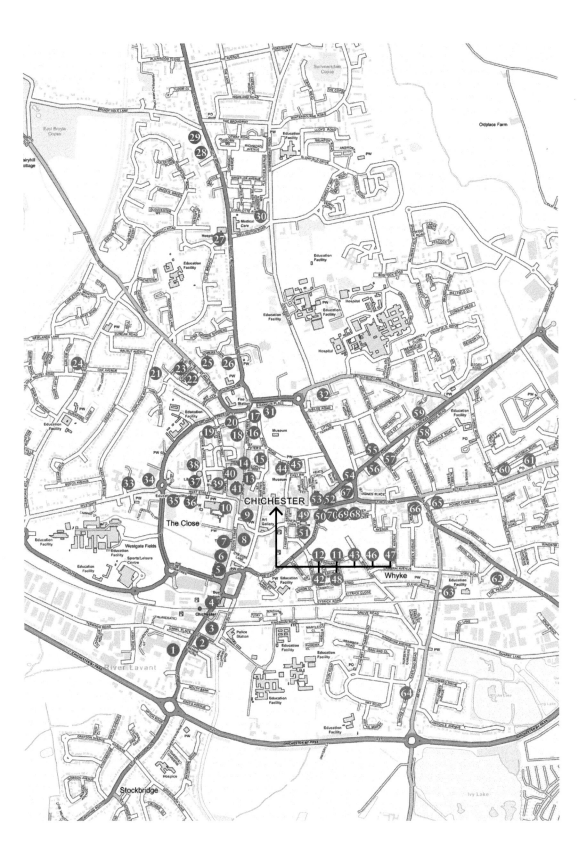

CHICHESTER PUBS

DAVID MUGGLETON

AMBERLEY

About the Author

Dr David Muggleton is a professional lecturer and writer with an interest in pub and brewery history. This is his third book with Amberley Publishing, the first two being *Brighton Pubs* (2016) and *Brewing in West Sussex* (2017).

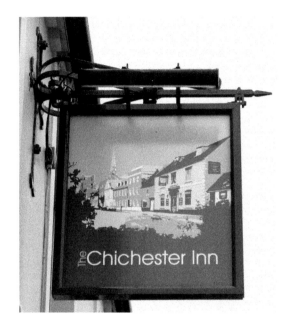

First published 2017

Amberley Publishing
The Hill, Stroud
Gloucestershire, GL5 4EP

www.amberley-books.com

Copyright © David Muggleton, 2017
Maps contain Ordnance Survey data.
Crown Copyright and database right, 2015

The right of David Muggleton to be identified
as the Author of this work has been asserted in
accordance with the Copyrights, Designs and
Patents Act 1988.

ISBN 978 1 445 6 7017 1 (print)
ISBN 978 1 445 6 7018 8 (ebook)

British Library Cataloguing in Publication Data.
A catalogue record for this book is available from
the British Library.

Origination by Amberley Publishing.
Printed in the UK.

Key

1. Gatehouse
2. Richmond
3. Railway Tavern
4. Foundry
5. Vestry
6. Chantry
7. Fountain
8. Trents
9. White Horse
10. Crown
11. Little Anchor
12. Wheatsheaf
13. Queen Anne
14. Old Cross
15. Park Tavern
16. Chichester Harbour Hotel
17. George & Dragon Inn
18. Foresters Arms
19. Nursery Arms
20. White Hart
21. Arundel Arms
22. New Inn
23. Angel Inn
24. Inn on the Green
25. Rainbow Inn
26. Bell Inn
27. Wellington
28. Inkerman Tavern
29. Old House at Home
30. Fleece
31. Sun
32. Hope Inn
33. Waggon & Lamb
34. Crate & Apple
35. Chichester Inn
36. Red Lion
37. Duke & Rye
38. Prince of Wales
39. Eagle
40. Belle Isle
41. Dolphin & Anchor
42. Royal Arms
43. Hole in the Wall
44. Crab & Lobster
45. Curriers Arms
46. Golden Cross
47. Prince Arthur
48. Fleece
49. Market Tavern
50. Cattle Market Inn
51. Bull Inn
52. Unicorn Inn
53. Nags Head
54. Black Horse
55. Victoria
56. Coach & Horses
57. Ship & Lighter
58. Star & Garter
59. Red Lion
60. Wheatsheaf
61. Barley Mow
62. Wickham Arms
63. Mainline Tavern
64. Crown Inn
65. Four Chesnuts
66. Blacksmiths Arms
67. Castle
68. Half Moon
69. Bush
70. Eastgate

Foreword

The following book names all pubs, inns and taverns that the author knows to have existed within the confines of the four walks that form the main chapters. All currently trading pubs are afforded a separate entry as are those that the author has classified as 'closed'. Closed pubs are those that are no longer trading but enough is retained of the site and building to warrant detailed discussion for the purpose of historical interest and architectural merit. What the author has alternatively classified as 'lost' pubs receive just a namecheck, mostly in the relevant chapter introduction. Lost pubs consist of those where the site cannot be identified for certain as well as those where the site is known but the original building has either been demolished or significantly reconstructed. Many pubs were lost before the commencement of street numbering and prior to the development of extensive and reliable methods of record keeping. Some street numbers given for lost pubs may therefore be approximations or even no longer pertain, while some dates provided may not be entirely accurate or account for the whole scope of the pub's existence. The distinction between closed and lost pubs is admittedly one of degree rather than absolute and the author may have on occasion erred in judgement one way or the other. While pubs were traditionally known under a sign and formally referred to by a name, such as the Kings Head, Fleece or Wheatsheaf, this was often not the case for alehouses and beerhouses. All beerhouses known by a name are mentioned in this book but hardly any of that majority recorded in directories or registers only under the personal name of the licensee, and for which just the unnumbered street location or general area is known. For premises with a separate entry in this book, the major part of any brewery ownership, where known, is identified by initials in brackets immediately following the address, unless this information is provided in the entry itself. The initials stand for the following breweries: B: Brickwoods; C: Constable; EA: Eagle; EW: East Walls; KT: Kemp Town; F: Friary; PBU: Portsmouth & Brighton United; R: Rock; SS: South Street; T: Tamplins; WG: Westgate. A dash between initials represents a process of acquisition. All these breweries are mentioned within the course of this book and the reader will find the penultimate paragraph of the following introduction to be particularly helpful in this matter.

Introduction

The county town of Chichester is the only city in West Sussex. Its origins lie in a fortified Roman camp, Noviomagus Reginorum. The Second Legion commanded by Vespasian invaded this part of the south coast in AD 43. Instead of meeting with resistance they received co-operation from the native Celtic chieftain Cogidubnus, who was afterwards appointed by the Emperor Claudius as Imperial King and Legate in Britain. The Romans encircled the camp by a defensive wall and erected four gates: at the north, south, east and west. These gates were demolished in the eighteenth century but significant sections of the wall remain, although largely rebuilt, and the grid pattern thus produced is still evident in the plan of the city today. The four main shopping streets are named after the cardinal points of the compass and intersect at the medieval Market Cross, erected by Bishop Storey in 1501. This street layout of a cross within a walled circle (the effect rather like cutting a round cake into quarters) also gives the city four relatively secluded quadrants, each bounded by two of the main streets. The Roman founders of Chichester feature on local history panels at the Lloyds No. 1 Bar, the Gatehouse. The ghost of a Roman centurion is said to haunt the Chichester Inn in West Street, and the Old Cross pub in North Street is thought to occupy the site of a Roman taverna, a gaming house where the favoured Roman tipple of watered wine was served.

It is unclear whether Noviomagus Reginorum became completely uninhabited and derelict after the Romans departed but the *Anglo-Saxon Chronicle* relates how it was captured around AD 477 by the invading Aella, who pronounced himself King of the South Saxons. Aella gave the settlement to one of his sons, Cissa, with the name Chichester deriving from it – Cissa's *ceaster*, or camp. The Saxons drank in communal alehouses but nothing remains of those simple wooden structures. Chichester became a cathedral city after the Norman Conquest. The see was transferred from Selsey in 1075 and much of the present cathedral building was in place by 1123. The Bishop of Chichester from 1245–53 was Richard of Wych. After his canonisation in 1262, pilgrims travelled in large numbers to worship at his shrine. Many local taverns would have catered for their needs but the earliest recorded here was the Tabard in 1440, the location of which is unknown, likewise that of the sixteenth-century Green Hat. The various offices of the cathedral also once held the freehold of many licensed premises. In South Street, for example, the vicars choral, who performed prayers and Masses, owned the White Horse, while the administrators, the dean and chapter, leased the Kings Head. The latter body also oversaw St Mary's Hospital in the north–east quadrant, whose custos owned the sites of several inns and beerhouses, such as the Black Horse in St Pancras.

The wealthiest town in Sussex in the medieval period, Chichester was an important commercial centre that held regular markets and had a significant proportion of merchants, many of whom traded in grain and owned malthouses. Given its location near the South Downs, the wool and cloth industries were well established, providing a prosperous living for mercers and drapers. Yet the gap between the rich and poor was more severely marked than in the surrounding countryside where the aristocracy and landed gentry gave patronage to the workers on their estates. Those engaged in the cottage industries of Chichester, such as needlemaking, perhaps sustained a standard of living not much above the poverty line. A range of licensed premises developed accordingly to accommodate the varying needs of the populace. Inns were the largest, purpose-built establishments, whose keepers provided plentiful refreshment, accommodation and stabling for travellers and hired out large rooms for meetings and functions. The much rarer taverns specialised in the retail of wine to a wealthy clientele. Humble alehouses, run by 'tipplers' or 'huxters', offered only ale and basic victuals, often from just one room of a private dwelling, and perhaps gave rudimentary lodging to the foot traveller. In 1574, Chichester had five inns and thirty-two huxters, vinters and victuallers. In 1604, there were seven inns and thirty-four alehouses and tipplers. There were still seven inns in 1651, plus forty-one alehouses and nine huxters.

Chichester is lauded for its elegant Georgian architecture largely because the city lagged behind in making the transition from timber to brick as building materials. Rather than employ brick as patchwork infill for wattle and daub as first happened elsewhere, the sustainable timber-framed buildings of Chichester were fully encased in brick from the early eighteenth century. For both the Fleece in East Street and the Kings Head in South Street, the jetty (overhang) of the upper floor was bricked-up and encroached into the street, while the refronting of the Royal Arms and the White Horse in those same two respective streets left them with residual jetties that remain to this day. Although the streets themselves were more sanitary than they had been in 1641 when John Combes, landlord of the aforementioned White Horse, was prosecuted for allowing 'his dung to be layed out against the Pallant Church', the pavements remained in poor condition. The Paving Commissioners were set up in 1791 to ensure their cleanliness, repair and removal of obstructions, the latter including projecting inn signs. The following year they ordered signs to be taken down from several public houses, including the Little Anchor and the Wheatsheaf – both in North Street. Also coming under their watchful eye was George Seymour, landlord of the City Arms in that same street. His propensity for putting out seats in front of his house for customers to drink at, particularly on beast market day, was regarded in 1829 by the commissioners as a 'frequent nuisance' and a 'great inconvenience' to the public.

The eighteenth and early nineteenth centuries were the era of the coaching inn. Sussex roads were once among the worst in the country and coach travel was not merely arduous but downright dangerous. Yet, from the middle of the 1700s, a local turnpike system led to better road conditions and improved coaching services. In 1784, the Chichester, Brighthelmstone and Portsmouth Diligence left the Unicorn Inn in Eastgate Square every Tuesday and Friday. The city was also on a secondary route for mail and post coaches, while the wagons of numerous carrier firms departed from the King of Prussia in Little London, the Ship & Lighter in St Pancras and the White Horse in Northgate, among others. The 1846 arrival of the railway in Chichester signalled the demise of these means of road transportation just as surely as it decimated the canal traffic. While the steam train gave commercial impetus to the category of house henceforth known as the 'railway inn', such as the Globe in Southgate, it equally diverted business from the coaching inns. In East Street, the once prestigious Swan did not adapt to changing conditions and was not long in closing, whereas the Fleece, in modern parlance, successfully 'downsized' to become a pub. In West Street, the Anchor and the neighbouring Dolphin began trading as 'commercial and family hotels' and boldly embraced modernity: the former became the meeting place of the Bicycle Touring Club, the latter the headquarters of the Royal Automobile Association.

In 1839, Chichester had six inns, thirty-four taverns and public houses and at least forty-four beerhouses. The latter were a creation of the 1830 Beer Act, and for nearly four decades remained outside the purview of the justices. While the number of licences continued to grow for the greater part of the nineteenth century, initially under the banner of 'free trade', countervailing tendencies were at work. Successive licensing acts from 1869 ended the era of unlimited expansion and gave greater power to magistrates to suppress pubs and beerhouses regarded as surplus to requirements in a given area. This signalled a victory for temperance agitators and it is a sign of the times that in the 1890s a coffee tavern started trading here in East Street and two temperance hotels were set up in Southgate – one near the Woodman Inn, the other next door to the Railway Inn. Writing at the end of that decade, the naturalist W. H. Hudson gave voice to the anti-drink lobby in recording his experiences of a visit to Chichester in tones too contemptuous to fully convey here. Suffice to say, seventy or so licensed premises were, for Hudson, far too many for the village-sized population of Chichester, particularly as the number of adult males (women, for Hudson, were ruled out of the equation) included a large body of clergy and other 'highly respectable' citizens who did not patronise bars. Those that did he described as 'the most utterly drink-degraded wretches it is possible to find anywhere in the Kingdom'.

Matters came to a head locally with the 1903 'massacre' of the city pubs, which saw seventeen licences simultaneously 'surrendered in pursuance of the agreement between the justices and the brewers'. Still another seventeen Chichester pubs shut in the period 1910–25 and a further eight in 1931–39. The police and justices continued to hold the balance of power when it came to bargaining with brewers over the surrender or continuation of their licenses, as evidenced by the 1921 sacrifice by Friary, Holroyd & Healy of their Curriers Arms for the Prince Arthur – both in Little London. Yet it would be over-simplistic to see the drink trade as a monolithic entity curtailed by punitive political legislation, for a powerful alliance of progressive policymakers and enlightened brewers had by this point emerged to advocate reductions in the numbers of poor quality pubs so that new ones could be built (or the older ones rebuilt) with better amenities that encouraged what would today be termed 'responsible drinking'. This gave rise to what became known as 'the improved public house movement' of the interwar period. Based on a philosophy of 'fewer, bigger, better', improved pubs often replaced outmoded premises, sometimes with the licence transferred from a house closed elsewhere, and perhaps with the additional agreement that a further licence would be surrendered. Respective examples of such improved pubs in Chichester are the Swan (now the Crate & Apple) in Westgate (1936), the Nags Head in St Pancras (1925) and the Hope in Franklin Place (1931).

By 1955, several decades of brewery mergers and takeovers had left the city's then forty-one pubs in the possession of just four breweries – none of them local. Gale's of Horndean and Brickwoods of Portsmouth each held a handful but the ownership of most Chichester pubs can be traced through the following chains of acquisition. The tied estate of the city's South Street Brewery was obtained in 1889 by the city's Westgate Brewery of Henty & Sons, who in 1921 acquired another five city pubs via amalgamation with Constable & Sons of Arundel and Littlehampton to form Henty & Constable. All brewing was transferred to the Westgate site, which eventually closed in 1955 and since then Chichester has been bereft of a brewery. The Westgate Brewery pubs were distributed in almost equal measure to Tamplins of Brighton (themselves already acquired by the London brewers Watney, Combe, Reid, subsequently Watney Mann) and Friary, Holroyd & Healy of Guildford (soon afterwards Friary Meux). That the latter then owned the largest proportion of the city's pubs was due them having in 1910 acquired the Eagle Brewery of Arundel from Lambert & Norris. This tied estate included Chichester pubs once owned by the city's East Walls Brewery in addition to those accumulated from previous owners of the Eagle Brewery. More consolidation through national conglomerates was to follow in the 1960s and 1970s when Watney Mann became part of Grand Metropolitan, Friary Meux was subsumed into Ind Coope under Allied Breweries, and Brickwoods was acquired by Whitbread.

Yet a radical transformation in drinking culture has been set in motion since the 1980s under the watchword of deregulation. Less than 40 per cent of the currently trading licensed outlets that feature in this book are owned by breweries or their subsidiaries. Virtually all the remainder are run by non-brewing companies, commonly called Pubcos. The unexpected 'microbrewery revolution' over the same period has nonetheless ensured that the overall choice of beers is greater now than when the traditional brewers held sway. That this author has now chosen to use the term 'outlets' rather than 'pubs' denotes the variety of drinking establishments that have sprung up to satisfy pluralistic tastes in a highly segmented market. This has undoubtedly had its downside. The decomposition of the manual working class has precipitated a sharp decline in the unreconstituted 'boozer'. Very few pubs closed in Chichester in the forty years prior to 1980, after which the rate has risen to rival pre-Second World War levels: only sixteen pubs now remain of the forty-one open in 1954 and a number of these have been rebranded. Conversely, hardly any additional pubs were built in the city for much of the twentieth century, whereas six new outlets have opened from 1997–2006. Traditional pubs still exist, such as the Eastgate in the Hornet. That it takes its place on this author's drinking circuit alongside the equally excellent Belle Isle in Chapel Street, which prefers to call itself a café-restaurant-bar, only serves to illustrate the positive aspects of the irrevocably changed drinking landscape of contemporary Chichester.

From the Canal Basin to North Street

Our first walk starts outside the old South Gate in Stockbridge Road. What was once an area of orchards, farm and meadowland has been fundamentally transformed by innovations in transportation: a turnpike road, the creation of the canal, the coming of the railway, the building of the bus garage and station, and the routing though Southgate of the A286 ring road – the latter stands on the sites of two lost pubs. On the west side of Southgate at No. 8 was the Railway Inn (1871–1903), subsequently Rugby House and now the Avenue de Chartres. On the east side at No. 34 was the Woodman Inn (1864–1935), subsequently the site of a garage and now the road gyratory system. We then stroll up South Street, which had few inns due to the unbroken rows of shops but also because much of the west side was under the ownership of the various offices of the cathedral. After we pass the Market Cross and enter the pedestrianised North Street it is a very different story.

North Street was the administrative centre of Chichester and is the site of the Council House and Assembly Rooms; the Market House also stands here and the main market was held in the southern half of the street. The roads that cross-cut North Street gave it the best communication routes across the city; hence it was a well-frequented area catered for by a number of inns and beerhouses. Lost pubs on the west side were No. 11, the Queens Arms in 1706, renamed the Kings Arms in 1714; No. 20, the Heart in Hand in 1839 and which became a wine and spirit merchants by 1922; No. 33, the City Arms (1811–1903), renamed briefly in 1845 during a period of 'ill conduct' as the Prince Albert; No. 44, the Star Inn in 1641; No. 46, the Bell (1780–84). On the east side, Nos 51–53 were the Kings Head Inn in 1592; at the Market House was the Crown Inn in 1574; next along was once an entrance to the Swan Tap, located behind the inn of that name in East Street; Nos 86–87 were the Bear Inn in 1670.

1. Gatehouse, Unit R4, Chichester Gate

J D Wetherspoon outlets are often conversions of redundant premises, but this Lloyds No. 1 bar of theirs occupies a newly built unit of 2003 on a leisure park – part of the development of a 'Southern Gateway' to the city. On the brick walls by the open staircase to the mezzanine floor are pictorial panels paying homage to the Roman

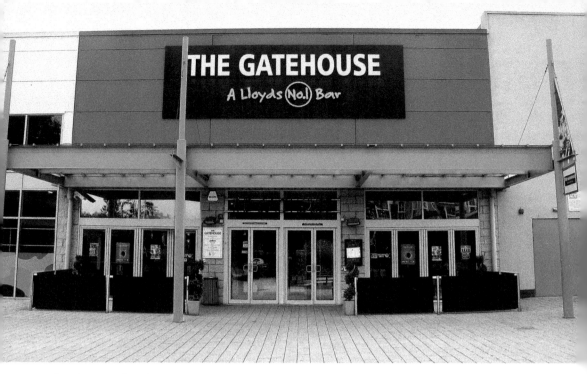

Gatehouse: Lloyds No. 1 Bar.

heritage of the city. The original intention was to call the outlet the Cissa Bar, so the Romans have emerged triumphant over the Saxons in this respect.

2. Richmond, No. 9 Stockbridge Road (WG-F)

In September 1987, George and Bob Arnold treated their mother, Mrs Winnie Gadd of Dorset, to a ninetieth-birthday surprise: a drive to this pub on the Canal Basin, where her father Marcus Heffer had been landlord from 1921–29. Winnie succeeded her husband Harold Arnold to the licence in 1938, remaining as landlady for fourteen years, having remarried as Gadd in 1942. During her nostalgic visit, Winnie was delighted to see that an old, bare-knuckled boxing poster put up by her father was still framed on the wall. This would surely have been the announcement of a sparring match that took place here on 2 July 1828 between 'Ned Neal and Whiteheaded Bob, assisted by Isle of Wight HALL and several amateurs'. The poster for this event stated that the two protagonists, 'Being recovered from their late Fight intend giving their Friends at Chichester a rare treat of the ART OF SELF DEFENCE'. The two performances – at 2 p.m. and 7 p.m. – were held in the 'Large Room' of the inn, with admission to each being 2s 6d.

The inn was built around 1821 to provide refreshment for bargemen and wharves workers. It takes its name (originally suffixed 'Inn', subsequently 'Arms' and now in the diminutive) from the Duke of Richmond, who in April 1822 launched his eponymous brig – the first vessel to be built at the Basin – just after the opening of this Birdham to Chichester part of the Portsmouth to Arundel canal line. A tragedy occurred here in 1833 involving five harvestmen who took refreshment at the inn after purchasing provisions in the city. The boat they engaged to row them back to their farm was overloaded and quickly

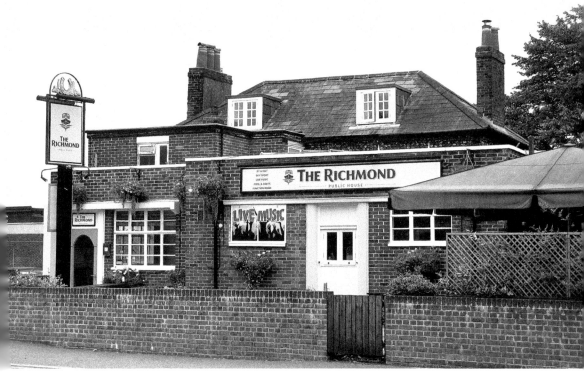

Above: Richmond front elevation.

Below: Richmond rear elevation.

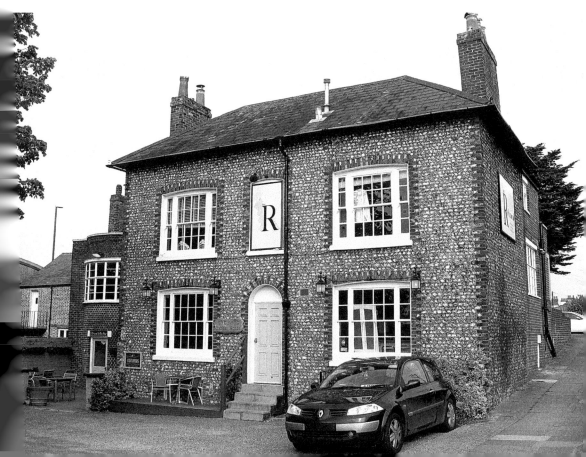

sank. Only the prompt attention of the inn landlord and a passing pedestrian enabled three of their party to be saved. A verdict of accidentally drowned was passed on the two young men named Morley and Redman. The heroic landlord may have been Clement Sayers, who was also a limeburner at a nearby pair of limekilns owned by the canal company.

The pub was radically reconstructed in 1937 to plans by architects Whitehead & Whitehead for builder F. Hill of Northgate and owners Henty & Constable of the Westgate Brewery. The only parts of the original flint-faced, slate-roofed premises (not Grade II listed until 1971) to escape demolition were the parlour and kitchen at the rear, which being down a slope are on a lower floor and now house the Snug Coffee Shop. On the Stockbridge Road side, the front wall of the old premises came up to the pavement line whereas the new building was set back 25 feet to form a car park, this surprising small space (car ownership was much rarer then) now taken by the patio. Whereas the old licensed premises ran west to east down Canal Wharf, the rebuilding realigned them north to south with a public bar, off-sales and saloon accessed through the still-extant three front doors. The pub spent some years as the Waterside before reverting to its original name by 2012.

3. Railway Tavern, No. 64 Basin Road (SS-WG-T)

This was the New Inn by 1839 under landlord William Thorpe, who died aged forty-six in 1841. As the inn name indicates, it was not the first in the vicinity: William and Maria Sweetman also had a beershop in Basin Road at this time. The renaming had occurred by 1847 after the arrival of the railway. Landlord Richard Combes was fined

Railway Tavern.

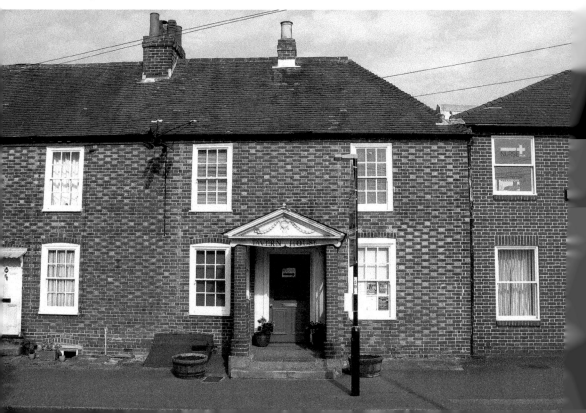

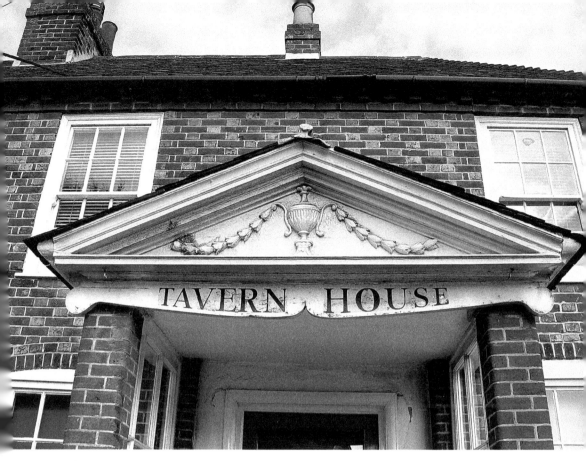

Railway Tavern portico.

in 1852 and again in 1859, having twice fallen foul of 1848 legislation requiring pubs to remain closed until 12.30 p.m. on a Sunday or until the end of divine service. The Railway Tavern closed *c.* 1970, but retains the wrought-iron sign bracket. Now named Tavern House, it forms part of a Grade II-listed terrace. Brickwork has replaced the stone columns that once supported the porch with its decorative portico.

4. Foundry, No. 1 Southgate (EA-F)

This occupies land once owned by the vicars choral, the northern plot of which was known as Stubbers Gardens. The southern part was previously the site of an iron foundry, so the new owners (Greene King Brewery of Bury St Edmonds, Suffolk) must have done their research before reopening the pub under its present name in 2016. The site was leased in 1836 to Stephen Purchase, who by 1839 had built what was at first called the Egremont Arms – after the third earl of that title who was the largest shareholder in the nearby canal. It became the Globe by 1845, probably in anticipation of the opening the following year of the neighbouring railway, for the name refers to the great globe of the earth itself and is a sign common to houses that cater for a cosmopolitan clientele. Three generations of the Purchase family held the lease of this important commercial inn and posting house until 1885, brewing there

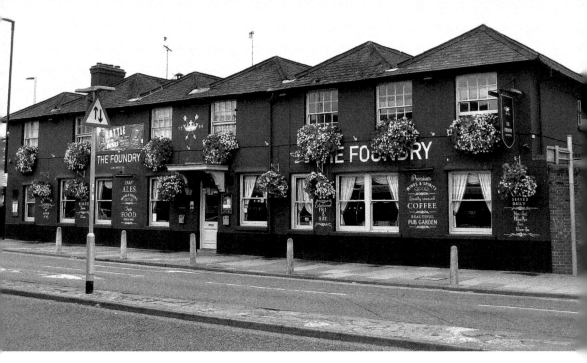

Foundry, formerly the Globe.

until *c.* 1878, after which they set up as wine merchants in North Street. From 1920 until the 1950s, the Globe operated as a managed hotel under Catering Houses Ltd, a subsidiary of owning brewery Friary, Holroyd & Healy of Guildford. From 1997 until its recent rebranding it was the epitome of the sports pub, with video gaming machines, a pool table and big-screen TV. It won the title of 'Best Sports Pub' in the 2011 Great British Pub of the Year Awards, the annual content organised by trade paper, *The Morning Advertiser*.

5. Vestry, Nos 21–23 Southgate

Opened in September 2000 by then owners Eldridge Pope under manager Marcus Tomkins, this occupies part of a conversion of a former supermarket that had been built in the 1980s on the site of a garage. The ground floor is a restaurant and bar with live sports on big-screen TV. Accommodation is available upstairs.

6. Chantry, Nos 27–28 Southgate

This 'urbanised pub' was opened on the ground floor of this property on Friday 23 September 2016. It was operated by the Stonegate Pub Co. under manager Neil O'Hagan and followed a £250,000 renovation and transformation of the former Slug & Lettuce pub that had been at this site since 2002.

7. Fountain, No. 29 Southgate (WG-F)

Since 1997, this has been a Hall & Woodhouse pub; the brewery trades under the Badger brand and is based at Blandford St Mary, Dorset. The Fountain spent a

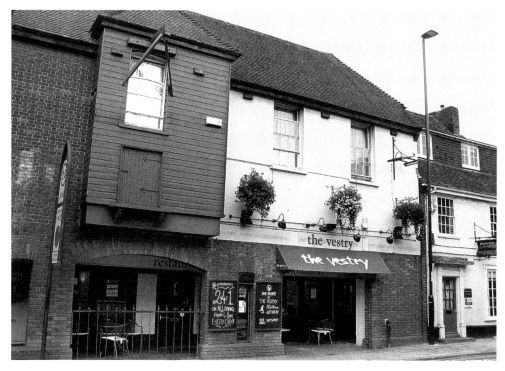

Above: Vestry.

Below: Chantry.

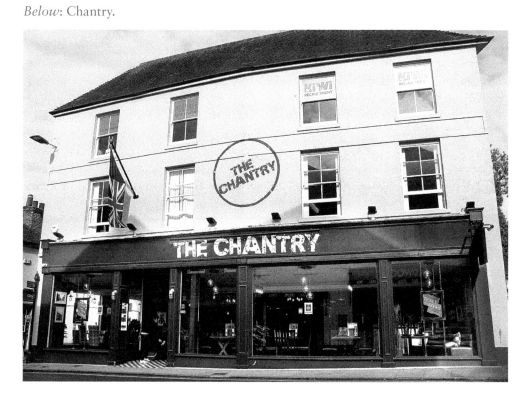

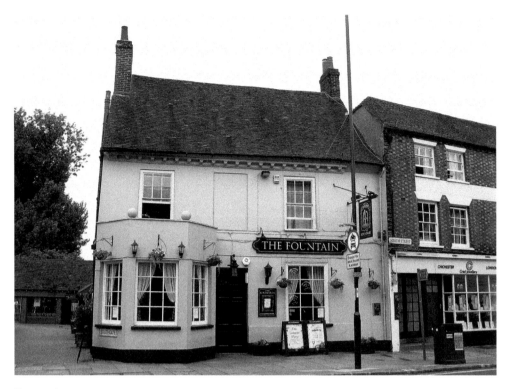

Fountain.

few years from the late 1980s as the Cathedral Tavern, before reverting to its original name. Its rear room was converted from a stable block in the 1960s. The Grade II-listed building is of the late seventeenth or early eighteenth century with its north end abutting the old site of the South Gate and part of the city walls. It became an inn around 1786 and was for some years a calling and receiving office for local carriers. In 1807, a shoulder of mutton of nearly half a stone in weight was eaten here in one hour for a wager by a private soldier, who also consumed 3 quarts of beer and wanted still more. In March 1813, Millington (alias the Muff) of Lavant beat Wheeler of Singleton in a contest of back-sword or single-sticks held in the yard. The landlord of the 1830s, George Neal, had a daughter named Sarah who married the professional Kent county cricketer Joseph Wells; their fourth and final child would grow up to be the famous writer H. G. Wells.

8. Trents, No. 50 South Street (WG-F)

The 250th anniversary celebrations of what was then the Kings Head were held in 1990 and led by landlord Andre Recknell JP, although an alehouse may have traded here as early as 1599. A succession of dwellings was known on this site from 1402, with a timber-framed construction eventually being enclosed by the present Georgian frontage. The building was Grade II listed in 1971. The landlady of 1769 was Cecily Gatehouse, who may have brewed at the back of the pub. Her son,

George, had acquired the South Street Brewery by 1828. A curious discovery made in an upstairs room during alterations of 1959 was a pull-down bed behind an alcove enclosed by a hinged door. It worked on the same principle as a modern version but was estimated to date from *c.* 1820, the time of landlord Henry Fogden, who was also a watch and clockmaker. On Monday 3 January 1848, landlord John Bilson hosted a ball here: tickets for ladies cost *2s 6d*, gentlemen paid *6d* extra – tea and coffee included.

The reminiscences of Mrs Iris Burgess, who used to live at the pub from the 1920s, featured in the local press of 1998. Her grandparents, George and May Drury, arrived at the Kings Head in 1906. After George died in 1920 her grandmother held the licence until incapacitated by arthritis. Iris's father George Styles, who had a been a welder in the garage behind the pub, then took over in 1931, but just over five years later died suddenly in bed from a stroke, aged fifty-one. Iris's mother Emily carried on to become the city's then youngest licensee and took the pub though the Second World War. In 1994 it became the Hogshead, part of the chain of Whitbread cask-ale houses of that name. This erasure of over two and a half centuries of history came under criticism from the Chichester Conservation Advisory Committee, who called it an 'unnecessary change for change's sake'. The pub was given its present name in 2005 when it became a Greene King tenancy and a non-smoking venue.

Trents, previously Hogshead, formerly the Kings Head.

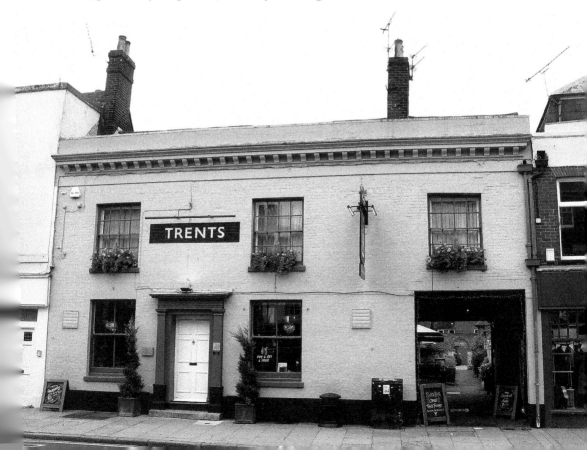

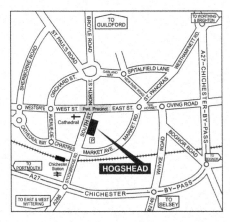
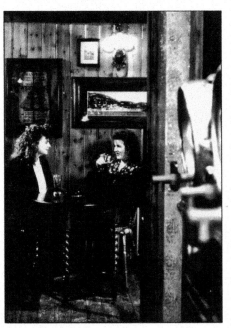
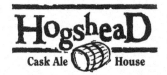
Hogshead flyer 1995. (Pub History Society Library)

9. White Horse, No. 61 South Street (KT-PBU-B)

Until its closure in November 2005, after which it became an Italian restaurant, this was the oldest trading city pub by a margin of two centuries. Behind the eighteenth-century red-brick frontage of the Grade II-listed building is a medieval timber-framed construction, evident from the beamed interior and overhanging first floor along West Pallant. A coroner's inquest of 1533 provides the first known reference to the inn by name. This was in regard to one William Skynner, who had been drinking and making trouble here with a tailor named Edward Holland. Skynner followed Holland outside and assaulted him by sword. The unarmed Holland was thus pursued until, in desperation, he struck Skynner on the head with a flint stone.

Skynner died three days later. Holland, who had taken sanctuary in the Dominican church, was later pardoned. The inn site was owned by the vicars choral, who by 1649 had leased the undercroft of the Vicars' Hall, opposite, to the innkeeper for use as a wine cellar.

   In the 1830s the inn doubled as the local excise office. For at least the second half of that century, the White Horse Tap stood at the rear of the inn where it adjoined the Parsonage House of All Saints, which was demolished in 1931. In leaded glass at this south–east corner of the premises is the KTB monogram of the Kemp Town Brewery of Brighton, owners from 1924–30 who added the attractive decorative windows of the front elevation and the Tudor doorway and herringbone brickwork along West Pallant. The architect was almost certainly John Leopold Denman. The inn has been the headquarters and meeting place of many diverse organisations: the Tradesmen's Club, 1836, who that year invited the Duke of Richmond to dine here with them; the Cyclists Touring Club, 1895; Oddfellows (Loyal Rock Lodge No. 967), 1909; RAF Association, 1954; Loyal Order of the Moose, 1958; Chichester Angling Society, 1962. A dark cupboard was even available here in the late nineteenth century for the use of amateur photographers.

White Horse front elevation.

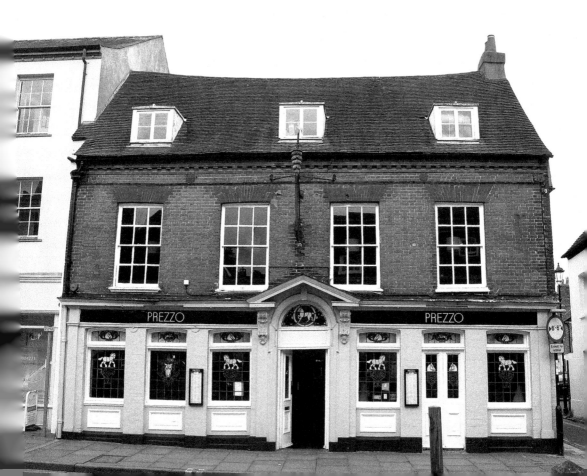

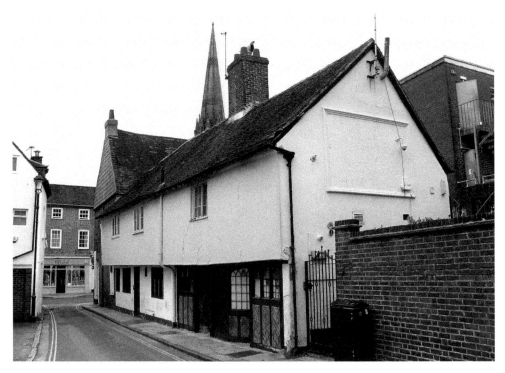

Above: White Horse West Pallant elevation.

Below: White Horse window, fitted late 1920s.

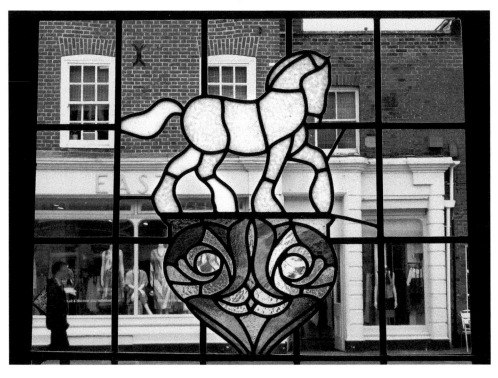

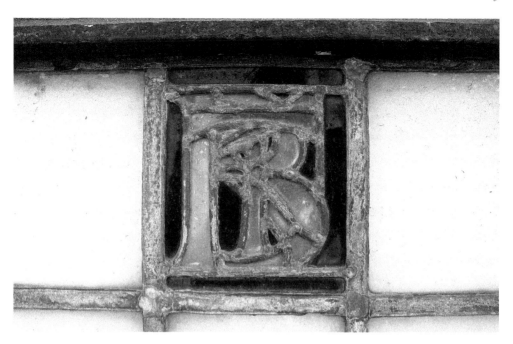

Above: White Horse, Kemp Town Brewery monogram.

Below: White Horse advert, *Moore's Chichester Directory 1880*.

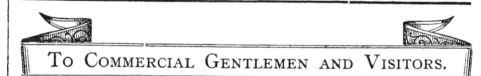

To Commercial Gentlemen and Visitors.

T. HOLMES,

WHITE HORSE HOTEL

(Opposite the Post Office),

SOUTH STREET, CHICHESTER

Well Aired Beds, with every attention to comfort and convenience.

WINES AND SPIRITS OF THE BEST QUALITY.

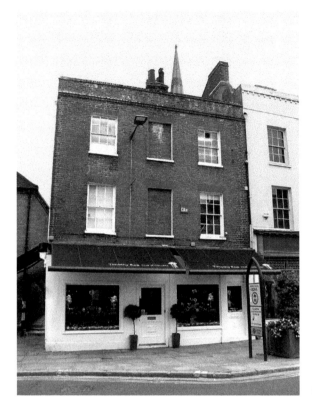

Crown (right side property).

10. Crown, No. 12 South Street (EA-F)

Nos 12 and 13 form a Grade II-listed eighteenth-century building, now trading as jewellers. By 1851, the northern half was a licensed eating house under James Alyward. It had a beer-only licence until 1924 when the renewal was refused and it became a florist. When the lightning conductor of the cathedral was replaced in 1884, the steeplejacks stayed here and it is said that they became 'well primed' in the bar before attempting their ascent.

11. Little Anchor, No. 85 North Street (WG)

This was open by 1784 under landlord William Holt; his widow Sarah continued to run these premises, in addition to the City Arms on the west side of the street, until shortly before her death in 1823 at the age of sixty. In 1849, Robert Thompson was committed to stand trial for theft of a bar of chocolate from landlord James Bridger. After the surrender of the licence in 1903, landlord Alfred Ainger moved north–west in 1905 to the hamlet of Hooksway and the Royal Oak. His son Alf married the following year and took over the Royal Oak the year after that and continued for over six decades. The Little Anchor was sold to a boot and shoemaker and still retails in footwear today. Behind the shopfront stands a timber-framed building. Renovations of 1990 received a Chichester City Council Blue Plaque Heritage Award. Nos 84–85 form a Grade II-listed pair.

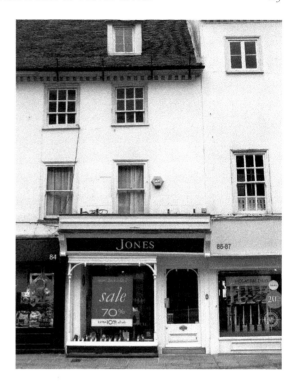

Little Anchor.

12. Wheatsheaf, No. 80 North Street (WG)

Previously the City Arms, by 1755 it was the Wheatsheaf, a timber-framed building that decayed to the extent that in 1804 it was rebuilt. The canted bays of the upper storey remain from that date. It became an important coaching inn with a large market room, dining room, several bedrooms and a goods yard with corn stores. Billiard rooms were a later addition to its facilities. A serious fracas occurred here on St David's Day of 1807 involving soldiers of the Monmouth and Brecon Militia stationed at the local barracks. They had been excused military duties for the duration but as the press report nicely phrased it, 'the harmony which prevailed among them in the morning evaporated towards the evening'. The constables were called and eventually restored order but not before one was bayoneted in the hand and another gentleman had three ribs broken. In 1830, a strong room was set up at the inn for the confinement of prisoners awaiting commitment for trial. More civilised times lay ahead and on 19 December 1888, hosted by landlord Ebenezer Taylor and under the auspices of the Local Volunteer Battalion, a Smoking Concert took place attended by a large and appreciative audience. Songs were sung, recitals given and a pianoforte skilfully played, all to an orchestral accompaniment. From 1894–1901 the landlord was James Lillywhite, nephew of Sussex county cricketer Frederick William Lillywhite, 'the nonpareil bowler', who owned the Royal Sovereign pub in Brighton. James was himself a talented player of the game; he visited Australia on six occasions and was known as 'the young nonpareil'. The licence of the Wheatsheaf was not renewed after 1915 and it was incorporated into a drapery. Nos 78–80 form a Grade II-listed trio.

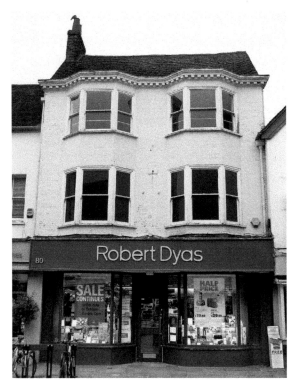

Wheatsheaf.

13. Queen Anne, No. 75 North Street

This was a beershop and eating house, probably by 1839 under brewer George Johnson, but certainly run for sixty-three years from 1845 by three generations of the Benham family. Benham's Dining Rooms, as the house was otherwise known, sold draught Worthington Burton Ale; also in the bar was a half-gallon tub of brandy that had been discovered by one of the Benham girls in the notorious smuggling spot of the Brandyhole Lane caves. The licence was dropped in 1913 and the premises became a bazaar. Nos 74, 75 and 75a form a Grade II-listed trio.

The Landlords
Reuben Benham (1784–1862) was landlord of the Fountain in Southgate from 1839–43, having taken over from his brother-in-law George Neal. The latter would not live to see the birth of his grandson, the writer H. G. Wells (1866–1946). (Wells was also the great-grandson of Reuben's own father, also named Reuben and drowned in a post-chaise accident in 1808.) In 1845, Reuben moved to the Queen Anne, which after his death was run first by his wife Ann. From 1868–80 it was run by his son George, then by an elder son – yet another Reuben and previously an omnibus conductor – until his death in 1900, and finally until 1906 by this last Reuben's son, William. Both William and his twin brother John died two years later at the age of forty-four. Mary Ann Benham, wife of the aforementioned George was probably the woman of that name who was landlady of the Crown Inn in Whyke Road in 1876–77.

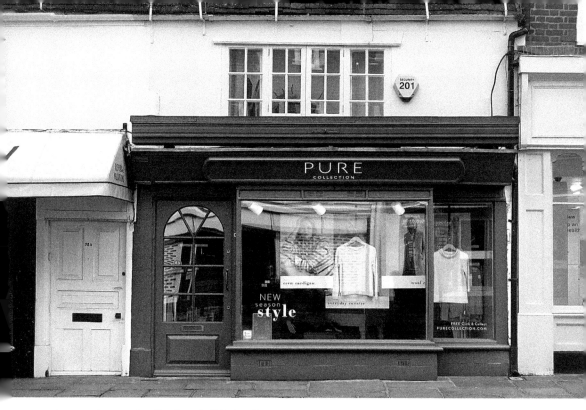

Queen Anne, aka Benham's Dining Rooms.

14. Old Cross, No. 65 North Street (T)

This mock-Tudor pub stands on land given to Bishop Arundel's chantry in 1501–02. It was the Green Dragon or Dragon in 1688 and the Dragon alehouse in 1753, becoming a pub under the present name (after the Market Cross) by 1872. From 1887–1918 the licence was held first by Arthur Purchase then his son Thomas George, wine merchants whose former premises stand opposite at No. 31. Ownership passed though a number of breweries to Smithers of Brighton, who demolished the old pub and in 1928 erected the existing half-timbered building with bold use of brickwork. The year is carved either side of a cross in a stone roundel to the left of the front door. Inserted around this date stone is a pair of dice, the faces showing a six and a five, the street number of the pub. These are Roman dice, according to some sources, and unearthed during subsequent renovations, thereby providing evidence for the theory that the original inn was constructed on the site of a Roman gaming house. Or perhaps the discovery gave rise to the supposition. Among the gouging in the roundel are what appear to be letters, but it is difficult to verify the assertion that these spell out the word 'temptation'.

During the late 1950s, under landlord Peter Bates, the pub was popular with city councillors and members of local organisations who no doubt enjoyed the grills in the Regency Buffet Bar and Tudor Dining Room followed by cocktails in the Mediterranean Lounge. A period of particular conviviality commenced in late-1963 with the arrival of George Allouis and his wife Laura from the London St James's restaurant Caprice, next to the Ritz. As a chef specialising in fish dishes accompanied by fine wines,

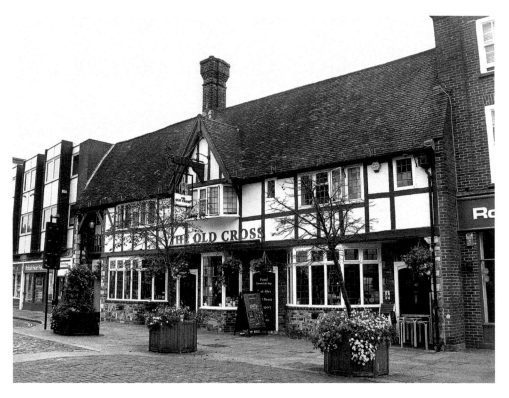

Above: Old Cross, rebuilt 1928.

Left: Old Cross date stone and dice.

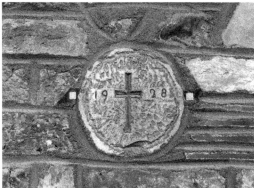

George attracted many of the big names in showbiz. The Beatles and the Rolling Stones dined here and it became a favourite haunt of actors appearing at the nearby Festival Theatre. Among the noted faces were such stars as Michael Wilding, Laurence Harvey, John Mills and Peter Ustinov. A special supper licence allowed George to entertain past the normal closing time until midnight. One patrolling policeman unaware of this extension knocked loudly on the door suspecting after-hours drinking. The story goes that as Sir Laurence Olivier was offering to clear the room, Billie Whitelaw re-entered assuring everyone that the situation was under control because Maggie Smith had taken the policeman away around the corner. George left the Old Cross in 1973, passing away eight years later, aged sixty-three, but had succeeded in (as Olivier put it) bringing the West End to Chichester.

The Landords
The newly arrived landlord of 1926, James Wolfe Hosgood, did not live to see the rebuilding of the Old Cross. In an era before penicillin, James died of septicaemia in the Royal West Sussex Hospital on 9 June 1927, aged just forty-one, leaving his wife Phoebe Elizabeth and children Doris, James Jr and Ivy. His gravestone in Chichester Cemetery is also engraved in memory of daughter Ivy who survived her father until 5 August 2005, just less than a month short of her ninety-third birthday.

15. Park Tavern, No. 11 Priory Road

Occupying a peaceful spot opposite Priory Park, the Park Tavern is first recorded by name in 1872 under landlord John Hughes. Before this date, however, Priory Road was called Priory Street and there were at least two beer retailers operating at unknown locations there, one of whom may have been a forerunner of the pub. The first known owner was John Parker of Midhurst, also proprietor of the Angel Hotel in that Wealden town with its steam brewery at the rear. In 1923, the Angel Brewery and its small estate, including this pub, were acquired at auction by Gale's Brewery of Horndean. Two years previously, however, the Park Tavern had been renamed the Ritz. It was the incoming landlord Thomas George Purchase, of the local family of wine merchants, who was responsible for

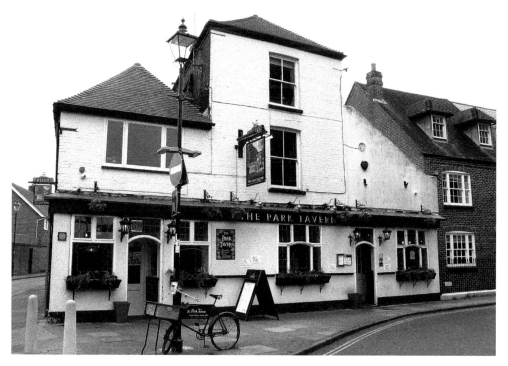

Park Tavern, once the Ritz.

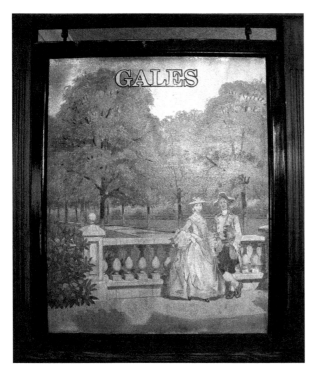

Park Tavern former sign.

what today would be called a rebranding exercise. The famous London hotel from which he took the name had then been in existence for fifteen years and was synonymous with impeccable standards of service, so unless some flippancy was intended (quite possible) one may assume this is what he intended to convey. By the end of that decade the Ritz pub was a meeting place for the charitable organisation Ye Ancient Order of Froth Blowers, whose beer drinking antics might involve jocularity but whose membership was never anything less than respectable. 'T. G.', as he was known to his family, was succeeded upon his death in 1953 by his son (George Arthur) Russell Purchase, who from 1950–51 had been Mayor of Chichester. During the 1950s the pub became a venue for traditional jazz at Club New Orleans, the resident band being Abe Aburrows Jazzmen. On 5 April 1964, the pub name reverted to the Park Tavern, some five months after Fred Taylor, who'd had both legs amputated, began his twenty-three-year stint as landlord. Since 2006, the pub has been owned by Fuller's Brewery of Chiswick, but the old Gale's sign is on display in the restaurant room.

16. Chichester Harbour Hotel, North Street

This building was at No. 57 until around 1964 since when it has carried no street number. As the Ship Hotel it acquired its first licence on 14 March 1939, held by Betty Healey, although it did not initially allow for bar or off-sales liquor purchases. David Guy, joint licence holder in 1977, was celebrated in CAMRA (Campaign for Real Ale) circles for being the first to bring to Chichester cask-conditioned beers brewed at Harveys of Lewes and King & Barnes of Horsham. For this achievement, the hotel was listed in the

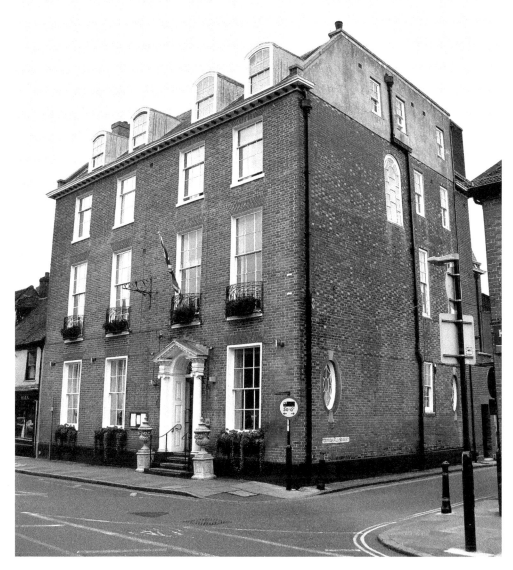

Above: Chichester Harbour Hotel, formerly the Ship Hotel.

Right: 'It must be Murray' at the Chichester Harbour Hotel.

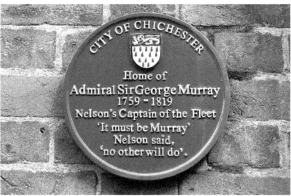

following year's *Good Beer Guide*. It was built 1804–06 as a townhouse for Admiral Sir George Murray (1759–1819), Captain of the Fleet to Admiral Nelson and Mayor of Chichester in 1815. The 217-dozen bottles in Murray's wine cellar realised £672 at auction after his death. From the late 1880s until 1919 it was home to Frederick Skaife, a surgeon at the Royal West Sussex Hospital, renowned for his pioneering operations on breast and ovarian cancer patients. William Seymour traded here as Guildhall Galleries from 1931 until 1938, when the premises were acquired by Allied Hotels of London who, in respect to its original owner, bestowed the nautical name.

To provide the additional accommodation, local architect Harry Osborn extensively extended the building to the rear, also adding the dormer windows along North Street and inserting the two oval windows with their fine batwing tracery on the ground-floor Guildhall Street elevation. The hotel's most famous guest was US General Dwight D. Eisenhower, who stayed for three nights while overseeing preparations for D-Day. A dinner in his honour was held at the hotel on the evening of 22 April 1944, attended by senior officers and top brass. Grade II* listed in 1950, the building was further extended at the rear in 1964 and 2001 and has had major internal alterations but retains notable original features such as a pedimented front door with ionic columns and fanlight; a fine staircase in the Adam style with cast-iron balustrade and mahogany handrail; and a four-bay arcade with palm-leaf and honeysuckle ornamentation on the first-floor landing. Since the liquidation of Allied Hotels in 1975, the hotel has seen a series of owners but retained the name of the Ship until its acquisition by Harbour Hotels in 2016. The blue plaque celebrating Admiral Murray was unveiled on 24 June 2013.

17. George & Dragon Inn, No. 51 North Street (WG-F)

This Grade II-listed building with a late nineteenth-century frontage was the Dog & Partridge in 1721 and the George by 1745, although it appears in the 1805 directory as the St George and under the ownership of Mrs Sarah Miller. She sold the freehold at auction in 1818, the particulars noting the house to have been established for nearly a century. The present name is first given in the 1832 directory under landlord Peter Pearson. Its spacious stable yard was probably used in the 1790s by carrier Robert Quennel, whose office was next door at No. 52. His waggons set out from Chichester to arrive at the White Hart Inn in the Borough, by which means large quantities of wool were conveyed to London and beyond. He also ran a daily post coach to the capital – calling at inns in Fleet Street, Westminster Bridge and Charing Cross – which passengers could use at their volition. The pub was a place of ill repute during the mid-nineteenth century and became popularly referred to as 'The Bucket of Blood' because of the fights that occurred on Saturday nights. Landlord William Payne was warned by the magistrates in 1849 for opening during divine service. In 1856, Adam Lintott regained his licence, having previously had it refused following complaints of late hours. By the time the Angel Provident Society met here on alternate Monday evenings in 1890, public houses had become more respectable and landlord Thomas Goldring was in the eighteenth year of his twenty-year tenure.

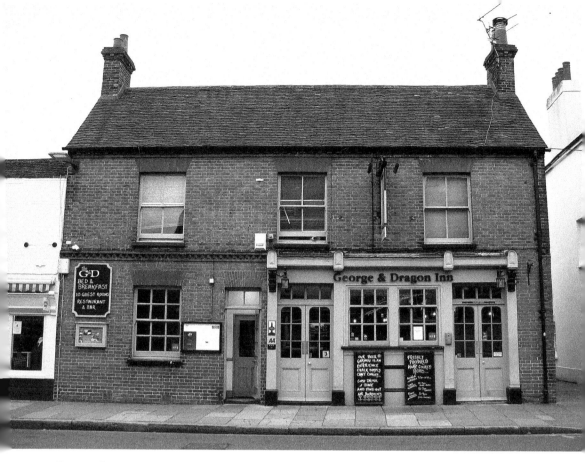

George & Dragon Inn.

The Landlords

Bernard 'Bobby' Reginald Burns sold his Bognor Regis joinery business to become a publican, taking the George & Dragon with his wife Pam in August 1977. A keen golfer and cricketer, he became scorer for Bognor Regis Cricket Club at the age of twelve, subsequently spending fourteen seasons as their umpire. He was also president of South Bersted Cricket Club and a member of Sussex County Cricket Club. Bobby played an active role in Chichester affairs, being a member of both the City Club and the Regnum Club. He co-founded the city's annual floral competition, winning first prize for best licensed premises in 1991. Having served as lance corporal in the Royal Sussex Regiment from the late 1940s, Bobby named one of the pub's drinking areas the Roussillon Bar after the city barracks of that name. Upon taking retirement in 1992, Bobby gifted all the paperwork concerning his time at the pub to the West Sussex Record Office.

18. Foresters Arms, No. 47 North Street (SS-WG)

Now tea rooms, this was the Foresters Arms beerhouse from 1862 until its licence renewal was refused in 1921. After the death of the first owner, George Langley, the licence was held for thirty-six years from 1877 by William Stoner. Nos 45–48 form a Grade II-listed quartet.

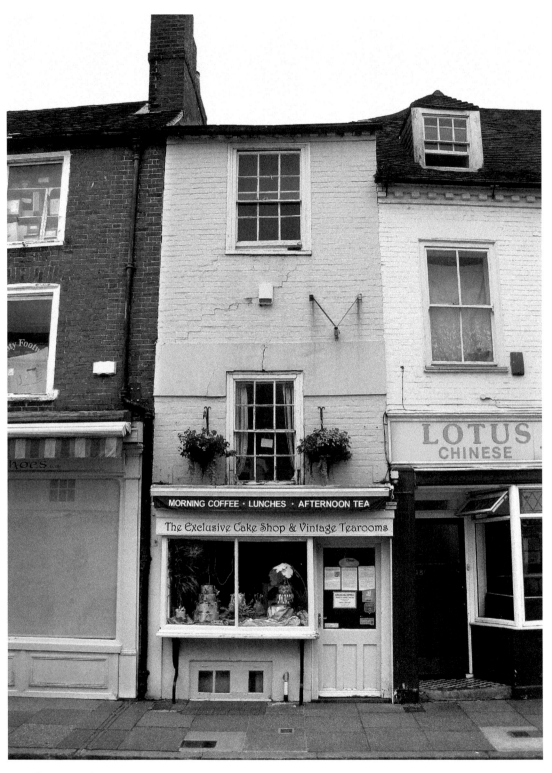

Foresters Arms.

2

Beyond the North Walls

We start this second walk in Orchard Street. Until the late eighteenth century this was an undeveloped lane amid orchards and arable land. A beerhouse at an uncertain location at what was then Orchard Terrace was the Beehive (1845–58) under Henry Triggs, dairyman, baker and retailer of home-brewed beer. Just outside the North Walls is Northgate, where the modern Metro House stands on the No. 11 site of the White Horse, known under that name by 1763 until its closure in 1935 and subsequent demolition following fire damage. It was originally the Queens Head (1701), then the Bear and probably also the Red Lion in 1740. We now make our way north–west along St Paul's Road, originally Old Broyle Road. The Broyle was an area of enclosed forestland and hunting ground. In the thirteenth century it was granted by Henry III to the Bishop of Chichester and eventually deforested, divided and leased out as farming plots. Development began here in the early 1800s of the Somerstown area and many attractive houses remain on the west side of St Paul's Road and in the part bounded by Washington, Cavendish and Parchment streets.

Much artisan housing in Somerstown between St Paul's Road and Broyle Road to the east was, however, demolished in the early 1960s in the name of 'slum-clearance'. Two pubs were closed under the scheme; also among the casualties were former pubs that had become shops or private residences – others had disappeared long before. None of the following now exist. At No. 74 St Paul's Road, on the south–west corner of High Street, the Waggon & Horses (1861–1962) once stood. In the no longer extant High Street itself: at No. 18 was the Good Intent (1815–1914), at the back of which was a bowling green; No. 30 was the Spotted Cow (1845–1925), and nearby in the 1860s was the Spotted Leopard. In Broyle Road (west side): at No. 4, on the north–east corner of George Street and next door to the still-trading Bell Inn, was the Beehive (1855–1935); No. 12, the Freetraders Hall (1839–1903); No. 15, on the north-east corner of High Street was the Star (1851–1962); somewhere before the site of the old infirmary was the Rose & Crown (1853–62); No. 55, the Duke of Edinburgh (1882–1903), which was very probably the same place as the Alma (known from 1859) and also possibly the Masons Arms in 1851.

Still on the west side, the precise locations of the following beerhouses once opposite the barracks are uncertain, but they ran south to north in this order up to Brandyhole Lane: the Dog & Partridge (1851–55), which was close to or possibly the same place as the Pointer in 1855–62; the Chinese Dragon in 1851, perhaps the same house as the Green Dragon (pre-1854); the Five Alls (1851–55). The barracks had the licensed Canteen, which was known from 1841–1903. Returning south, a brief detour eastward is now required down Wellington Road, after which further down the east side of Broyle Road, once opposite the old infirmary at No. 160 but now the bereft-of-buildings western border of Oaklands Park, was the Military Arms (1884–1903) – this was almost certainly the same beerhouse as the Britannia, which was known from 1842. Other lost beerhouses of Somerstown were the Dolphin (1864–66) under George Harding, location unknown, and the only reference to the Little Bo Peep is in an electioneering paper of 1830. After arriving again at Northgate we make our way east along Franklin Place to the bottom of College Lane to view two closed pubs, which then concludes this walk.

19. Nursery Arms, No. 186 Orchard Street (EW-EA-F)

This was a beerhouse by 1867 at the then Orchard Terrace, but could have been established anything from ten to thirty years earlier. It took its name from the seed and flower nurseries in the area during the nineteenth century. The landlord from 1880 until his death at the age of sixty-three in 1901, was the delightfully named Charles Henry Sweetlove. His wife Leah held the licence for two years afterwards. They had married late in life in 1896 and she

Nursery Arms.

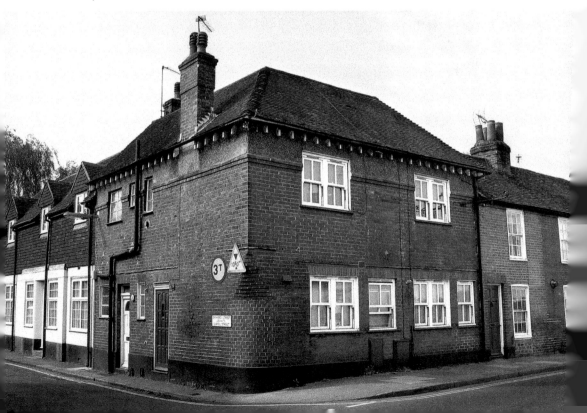

was aged around fifty-seven upon her death in 1905. Friary, Holroyd & Healy carried out alterations and additions to the pub in 1935 after it had received a full licence following a transfer from the closed White Horse in Northgate. In the 1950s it was a pub with a working-class clientele and paid out a tontine worth £1,000 at Christmas. It closed in 1982 under landlord Maurice Bowden, who had previously been at another pub shut by Friary Meux: the Prince Arthur in Little London. The wrought-iron sign bracket still remains and the building is part of a Grade II-listed terrace.

20. White Hart, No. 202 Orchard Street (SS-WG)

Previously the Jolly Sawyers (also known as the Sawyers Arms at an early stage), this was trading by 1839 at what was then Orchard Terrace. It appears to have been a particular disreputable pub during that period. The landlord of 1843, James Muggridge, was fined for permitting drunkenness and disorderly conduct in his house; the severity of the offence can be gauged from the sentence of one month imprisonment as an alternative to payment of the fine. The wrath of the magistrates was also felt by Muggridge's successor, James Jelliff, who in 1849 was admonished as to the conduct of his house in the future. In 1878, the pub was renamed the White Hart. The landlord of 1883–94, Richard Hall, also operated a bakery on site. The license was surrendered in 1903. The building is part of a Grade II-listed terrace.

21. Arundel Arms, Nos 21–22 Cavendish Street (EW-EA)

This is part of a Grade II-listed terrace that was erected in 1823 by Charles and James Farndell. It is unclear if this was the same site as the Beehive, recorded in this

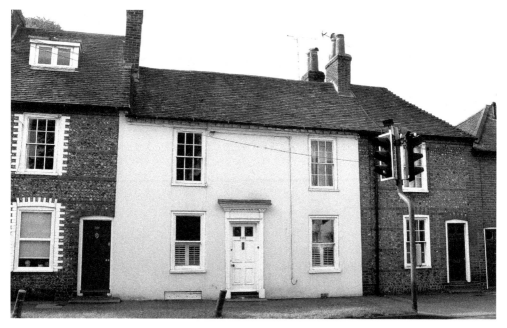

White Hart, formerly Jolly Sawyers.

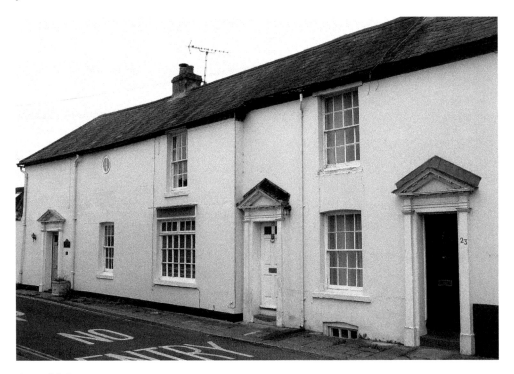

Arundel Arms.

street in 1844–45. Bricklayer Adam Janman was certainly a shopkeeper here in the 1840s, as his name can still be seen on a sign over the window. By 1855 it was a beerhouse under John Rossetter, who in June 1863 was fined for selling beer at 3.20 p.m. (A Sam Rossetter had been a beer retailer at an unknown location in Somerstown in 1839.) A valuation of 1867 noted the property to have consisted of basement cellars, an entrance passage, front parlour and front shop with a taproom at the back and a large smoking room, washhouse and three bedrooms on the first floor. It remained in the Rossetter family until 1888, John being succeeded first by wife Ann, then daughter Lucy. The name of the Arundel Arms was only acquired during the time of landlord John Guscott (1888–1910), when ownership passed to Lambert & Norris of Arundel. It closed after the final landlord Walter Rodgers had his license renewal refused in 1914. Afterwards he went into army service for the First World War. His family had moved to the Arundel Arms from the Balls Hut at Fontwell, where they had 100 grandfather clocks.

22. New Inn, No. 53 St Paul's Road

This house, on the corner with Washington Street, was built in 1827 by James Farndell. From today's perspective, it appears quite a grand place in which to have entertained persons of bad character and allowed drunkenness, two offences for which owner and licensee James Muggridge (also a dairyman by trade) was charged and fined in 1854. He had previously been at the City Arms in North Street, where was warned as to the conduct of his house and only retained his licence following an appeal from the brewer-owner.

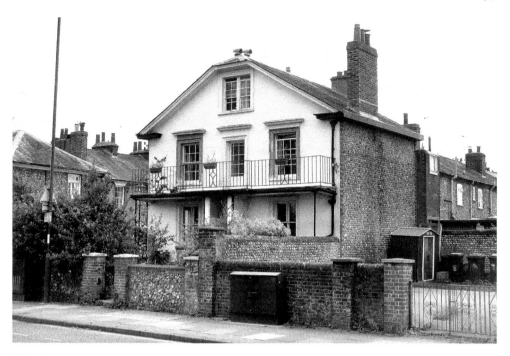

New Inn.

Before that he was at the Jolly Sawyers in Orchard Terrace, where he had been fined for a similar offence. This had become the New Inn under the Muggridges by 1851 and possibly as early as 1847. Upon James's death in 1856 at the age of forty-three, his widow Eliza carried on until her own death in 1874. The valuation of that year for the probate showed the extensive three-storey property to be fully furnished. On the ground floor next to the taproom was the bar, in which the inventory poignantly recorded an oil painting in a gilt frame titled *Virgin and Child*. Also here was a three-pull beer engine in an oak case alongside four spouted stone quart beer mugs and six straight of the latter, eleven spouted stone pint beer mugs and seven straight of the latter, plus a pewter quart, a pint and a half-pint. This is some twenty years before the beer glass begins to become popular and around a half-century prior to its mass production. The basement consisted of a kitchen, scullery and a cellar, the latter still containing around 54 gallons of beer. The house was sold the following year to Sharp Garland, a prosperous local grocer who went on to become twice Mayor of Chichester. By 1887 it was Fernhurst Lodge and the residence of Henry Harmsworth Jr, formerly of the Angel Inn at No. 57. It is now Grade II listed.

23. Angel Inn, No. 57 St Paul's Road (C-WG)

The house was built in 1811 by Robert Mason on land leased from Richard Dally. Two years later it was bought by Charles Austin Jacques, who in 1799 had been a brewer in St Pancras. It was purchased from Jacques in 1846 by Henry Harmsworth, who later erected a brewery and piggeries at the rear and had previously come into possession of two neighbouring cottages. By 1851 he was a brewer and beer retailer here and a

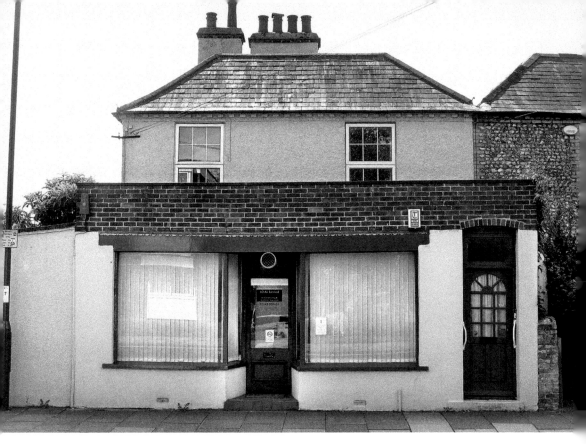

Angel Inn.

licensed victualler in 1863. He was succeeded on his retirement by his son of the same name, although ownership of the inn had been transferred by 1872 to Fred Temple, who lived in nearby Ellerslie House. The Somerstown Sick & Dividend Society held their meetings at the Angel in 1890. After forty years of a constant succession of licensees, it closed in 1923 after the last landlady, Eliza Tyms, had her licence renewal refused. A shopfront was subsequently affixed to the premises, partially obscuring the old house.

The Landlords
Henry Harmsworth the Elder was baptised on 23 August 1818 in Chichester. Ann Harmsworth (daughter of Henry Harmsworth, a gentleman's servant living in the parish of Funtington, Chichester) was baptised on 3 October 1838 in the parish of Rumney, Monmouthshire. The officiating curate Mr Jones afterwards added the name Ann Voller in darker ink directly over that of Henry Harmsworth in the baptism register. Henry Harmsworth married Ann Voller at the parish of Funtington or nearby Westbourne in the summer of 1841. The 1851 census has Henry as a master brewer living in St Paul's Road next to the Angel with his locally born wife Ann, their three daughters (the eldest recorded as Ann Harmsworth Voller, born in Monmouthshire), one son (Henry Jr) and eighteen-year-old domestic servant Lucy Rossetter, who thirty-six years later became the landlady of the Arundel Arms in close by Cavendish Street. Two

dates are given for the death of an Ann Harmsworth in Chichester: the fourth quarter of 1858 and, more precisely, 4 January 1859. On 4 January 1860 at the Parish Chapel of St Pancras, London, Henry remarried. It seems to have been the second marriage for his second wife, who was also named Ann. Henry Harmsworth died aged fifty-one on 24 February 1869, long before his second wife, who ended up living with her stepson Henry Jr and his family before passing away at the age of eighty-three. The William Harmsworth who in 1899 was running a temperance hotel at No. 10 Southgate, Chichester, seems to have been from another but not-too-distant branch of the family.

24. Inn on the Green, Oliver Whitby Road (B)

Under landlord Reginald Victor Nelson Endersby, this opened on 15 October 1957 as the Mitre. It was newly built for Brickwoods Brewery of Portsmouth to cater for the residents of the Parklands estate. One source states it to have been the first new pub in Chichester for nearly eighty years, but does not provide a precise date or a name for the previous claimant to this title. This author might respectfully modify the statement to suggest that the Mitre may have been the first newly built pub (i.e. not rebuilt on or near the same site) with a new licence (i.e. additional and not transferred or upgraded), perhaps since the early 1870s – nearly ninety years. The Mitre is not an uncommon name for pubs in cathedral cities, but it was renamed the Inn on the Green between 2009 and 2011 when it was closed and converted into a convenience store.

Inn on the Green, formerly the Mitre.

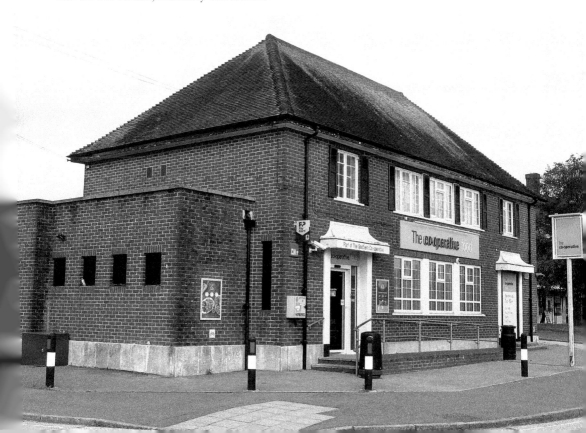

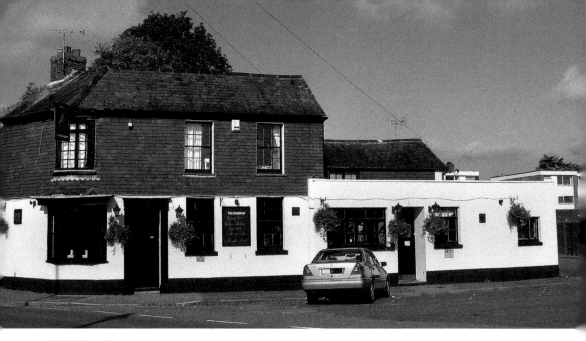

Rainbow Inn.

25. Rainbow Inn, No. 56 St Paul's Road (EW-EA-F)

This was in existence by 1839 under landlord Charles Matthews. By 1841 it was in the hands of the Stoneadge family, whose members continued to run it for the next forty-two years. Indeed, the house exhibited a remarkable stability behind the bar for over the first half of its history, for it had just five licensees during the course of the eighty-five-year period from April 1861 to February 1946. It is now one of only two pubs left in the Somerstown area of the city. Local resident Joyce McKenzie recalls that it once had an off-sales counter where children could buy chocolate, crisps and lemonade. For several years from the mid-1980s the pub excelled under Keith Dixon who, to the delight of the local CAMRA members, always had an interesting guest beer on handpump. In 1988, with his typical wit and humour, Keith entered his three-legged dog Nancy into the Friary Meux three-legged charity race across the city. The pub was called the Happy Medium for several years from 2006 before reverting to its original name, which according to the pub website is after the rainbows that can be seen above the building when looking north towards the Trundle, the site of an ancient circular fort.

26. Bell Inn, No. 3 Broyle Road (R-PBU-B)

The inception of this pub can be dated to July 1869 when James Harding gave notice of intention to apply for a certificate. It was initially known as the Blue Bell and stood opposite the poorhouse, now known as Cawley's Almshouses. The pub was run by the Harding family until 1896 and became part of the estate of the Black Lion Brewery of Brighton, who traded under the name of former owner William Chapman. During a repainting of the exterior in April 1962, a fascia advertisement was uncovered for Chapman & Co.'s Brighton Pale and Mild Ales and Double Stout. The fate of the Bell, along with that of the next door Beehive and the nearby Star, was held in the balance

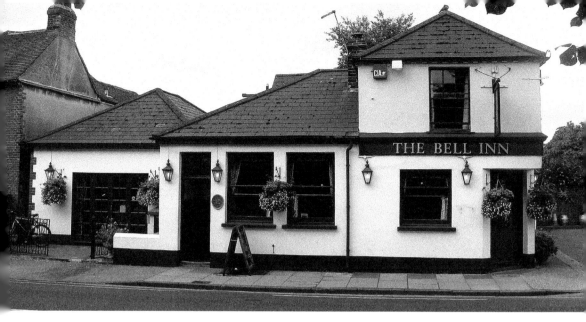

Bell Inn.

on Saturday 10 March 1910. During a tense meeting that morning the licensing justices made their case for there being too many licensed premises in the area, but the solicitors representing the breweries argued the merits of their respective houses and all three licences were renewed. In the 1950s, the Bell was fondly remembered for selling bottles of Portsmouth & Brighton United Breweries' Pompey Royal, a powerful, full-bodied, golden ale with an original gravity of 1060°. The Bell has been popular with the Festival Theatre crowd since the latter was opened in 1962. The public area of the pub was doubled in 1989 by a new extension to the south. It is one of only two surviving pubs in the Somerstown area and is on the City of Chichester Local Buildings List.

27. Wellington, No. 67 Broyle Road (WG-F)

This was the Lord Wellington in 1813. For most of its time it was called the Wellington, but was also known periodically as the Wellington Arms, the Duke of Wellington's Arms, and the Duke of Wellington. Being near to the Gallows Field at the Broyle, the inn must have enjoyed a roaring trade for the 'morning drop' of soldier John Holloway on Monday 26 October 1818 when a crowd of around 10,000 gathered for the ghoulish spectacle. Holloway had been convicted of the murder of Private James Parr, whom he had attacked outside the Anchor Tap in Upper West Lane, now Chapel Street. The inn is also just a short distance south of Brandyhole Lane, which as the name suggests was a notorious spot for concealing contraband. During the time of David Nettlefold, landlord from 1848–57, the inn was prone to searches by customs officers. An oft-told story of one such raid relates that, although nothing was discovered, Mrs Mary Nettlefold had been sitting quietly throughout the search, attending to her needlework with small barrels of smuggled liquor secreted under her voluminous skirt. The inn appears to have afterwards slumbered through an uneventful history. In 1987, it was the bimonthly meeting place for the Old Comrades of the Royal Sussex Regiment. It closed in 1990 and

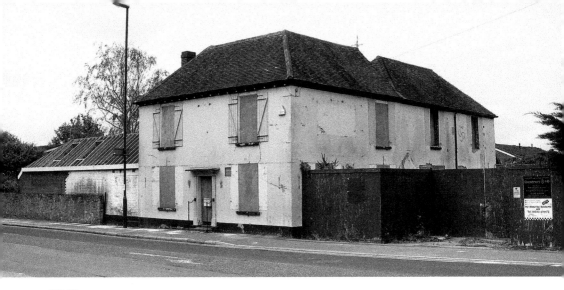

Wellington.

reopened the following year as a continental-style restaurant. An Inglenook fireplace was uncovered during the conversion of the building. The restaurant closed a few years ago and the house presently stands empty and shuttered, but provides a landmark opposite Wellington Road and is on the City of Chichester Local Buildings List.

28. Inkerman Tavern, No. 143 Broyle Road (WG)
The Battle of Inkerman (part of the Crimean War) took place on 5 November 1854 and this tavern opposite the barracks is first recorded as such in an 1858 directory under

Inkerman Tavern (right side property).

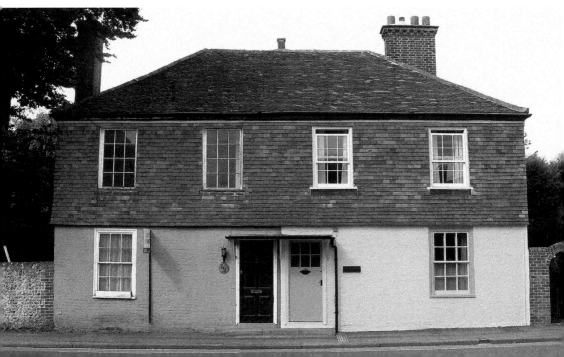

landlord John Gough. An 1872 valuation of the property included a six-pull beer engine and a skittles alley. The license was surrendered in 1903 under Mrs Martha Jane Clarke. She had been landlady here for nine years and afterwards moved to the Good Intent in George Street until it closed after her licence renewal application was refused in 1913.

29. Old House at Home, No. 145 Broyle Road (WG-T)

Also opposite the barracks, this was known from 1866 under the Goldie family, who continued to run it for the next half-century. It remained a beerhouse until February 1935, when a full license was transferred from the Woodman Inn in Southgate. It had closed by March 1996 and was subsequently converted into a private house.

30. Fleece, No. 27 Wellington Road (WG)

This old property is known on its Grade II-listing citation as the Beacon. That the roof line is considerably lower at the east suggests it may have originally been two separate cottages. From at least 1825–62 it was known as the Fleece at the Broyle or the Golden Fleece, or alternatively the Elm or Elm Tree, for it stood in the shade of an ancient elm around which people sat on seats. It was famed for its blood sports such as bull-baiting by bull terriers, cockfighting and single-sticks. The latter has been described as a sport where two men beat each other with cudgels with their free hand tied behind their back. The winner was deemed to be the one who first opened up a wound on his opponent's forehead from which the blood ran for more than one inch. A butcher of Wiltshire is reputed to have cracked open fourteen heads in one day here. The landlord, Daniel King (1783–1836),

Old House at Home (left side property).

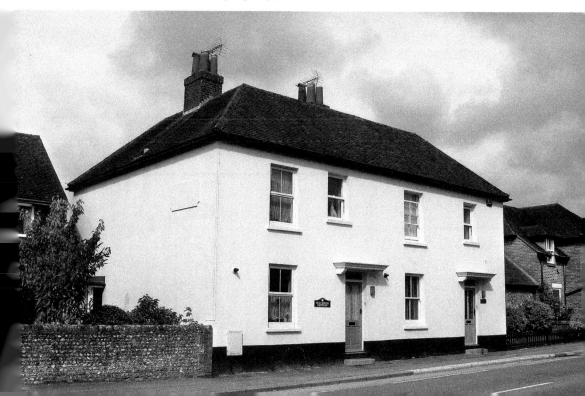

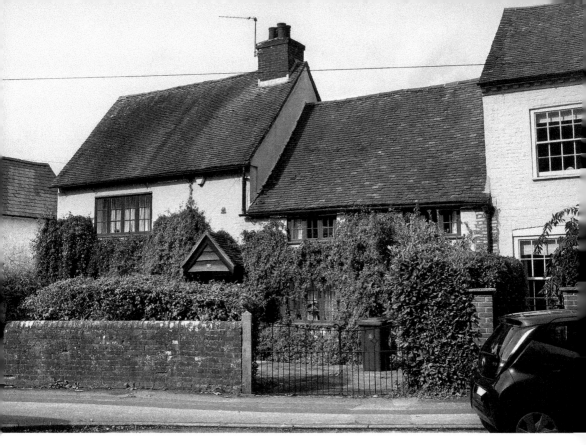

Fleece (at the Broyle).

was a first-class cricketer and member of the MCC. His attire included a silk handkerchief embossed with the laws of the game. It was afterwards framed in the pavilion of the Sussex County Cricket Club. His widow Mary carried on the inn after his death and on Thursday 23 November 1843 hosted the annual festival of blacksmiths, attended by some thirty of their trade – this being the day of St Clement, their patron saint.

31. Sun, No. 1 Franklin Place (EW-EA)
Of flint construction behind the rendering, this Grade II-listed building was once the home of David Goodman (1918–2013), a trained artist and newspaper columnist who was not only instrumental in the creation of the Chichester Festival Theatre but was the founder in 1973 of the Chichester Society, which campaigned for the preservation of the city's architectural heritage. David led highly publicised protests against the demolition of many old but otherwise fine buildings during that decade, when a concern for conservation was still regarded by the powers that be as subordinate to the driving force of progress.

Testimony to the former name and use of this particular house is the small carving of a sun on the front window lintel. A valuation of 1867 recorded the licensed premises to have consisted of a bar parlour, taproom, smoking room and club room on the ground floor. What is now the garage used to be a forge and the two occupations of publican and blacksmith were combined here by William Cates in the late 1880s. It was

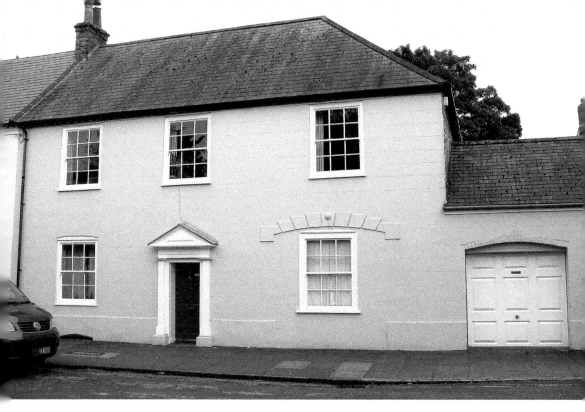

Above: Sun.

Below: Sun forge advert, *Moore's Chichester Directory 1887*.

WILLIAM CATES,

𝔓ɾɑctɩcɑl 𝔉ɑɾɾɩeɾ,

" SUN " FORGE, Franklin Place, CHICHESTER.

——o——

Horses shod with all the latest improvements.

All kinds of General Smith's Work executed on the shortest notice.

originally called the Woolpack and known by 1839 under landlord Charles Knight, who in 1843 was fined for permitting drunkenness on the premises. It was renamed the Sun in 1845 and witnessed a steady turnover of publicans until the surrender of its license in 1903. Renovations in 1999 revealed painted letters below the first-floor windows advertising 'ATKEYS XX & XXX ALES', a remnant of the 1860s–70s when the pub was part of the tied estate of Atkey's East Walls Brewery.

32. Hope Inn, Spitalfield Lane (F)

This opened in early 1931 under landlord George Weller at what was then called Franklin Place. It was a new build for Friary, Holroyd & Healy, with the licence transferred from an inn of the same name in St Pancras that was closed and subsequently demolished. It was also a condition of the licence that the opening of the new Hope would require the closure of the Dell Hole beershop next door at what was then No. 50 Franklin Place. This had been retailing beer since at least 1839 and was so called after the shallow pond at the south–west corner of College Lane. It became a private house and was demolished in 1967. The Hope was converted to a convenience store in late 2013.

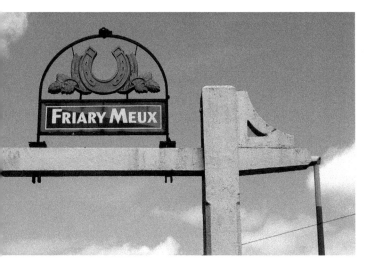

Left: Hope Inn, Friary Meux horseshoe, since removed.

Below: Hope Inn.

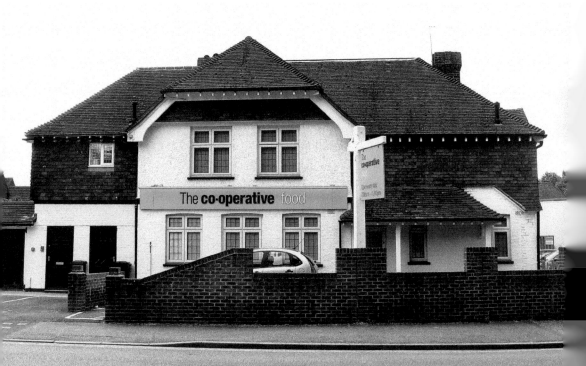

3

From Westgate to East Street

This walk commences in Westgate, where a suburb was developed from the thirteenth century. The area sustained damage in the Civil War and one of the buildings destroyed in the conflict was the White Horse Inn, which was rebuilt before 1673 and closed *c.* 1900. It stood on the south side at No. 3 and was demolished in the early 1960s for the Avenue de Chartres. Two lost inns on the north side before the site of the current Crate & Apple were the Ship in 1672 and the Three Tuns in 1688.

We then walk up West Street, a wealthy residential area of elegant houses. It also affords an uninterrupted view of the cathedral, although this was not always so. Before 1852, what is now the pavement on the south side in front of the cathedral grounds was occupied by a row of properties including three inns: at the west, the Sun in 1680, known for a period until 1800 as the Coach & Horses; in the middle, the Star in 1623, renamed the Royal Oak by 1813; at the east, the Crown in 1621, also known 1811–13 as the Crown & Sceptre. The Royal Oak was resituated on the opposite (north) side of the street at No. 12; it closed in 1903 and was demolished in 1962. The Boot alehouse was around this site in 1682.

The north–west quadrant once consisted of market gardens, granaries, slaughterhouses and small holdings but was redeveloped from the 1960s. Few old residences remain and all but the last of the following pubs have been pulled down. Tower Street on the west side at No. 10 was the Ship Inn in 1734, rebuilt in 1880, demolished in the mid-1960s and now the site of the public library; a few doors further north was the Olive Branch in 1856. On the east side, at No. 50 was the Fighting Cocks (1760–1900), which was demolished in 1911 and now the site of the new city museum. On the west side of Chapel Street, at No. 10, just south of Providence Chapel, was the Woolpack (1839–1901). On the east side at No. 15, just north of Crane Street, was the Butchers Arms (1855–1936). The next three were south of Crane Street: at No. 20, the Three Tuns Inn (1804–1910); No. 22, Royal Sovereign (1861–1903), demolished *c.* 1935; Nos 24–25, Sussex Arms (1870–1903). In Crane Street was the Victoria Arms (1859–61) on the still-extant north side – probably at No. 3.

We pass the Market Cross and enter East Street to find it completely bereft of pubs. This was not the case so long ago but always predominant along this stretch have been shops and banks. One of the latter stands at Nos 5–6 on the site of the Swan Inn, once the city's most prestigious and important hostelry. Known by 1527, it was rebuilt in the early 1700s and again in 1813 following a fire. It closed soon after 1845 and was demolished in 1897 after another fire. The Swan Tap at the rear survived until at least 1861. Also lost on this north side were: No 23, the Red, White & Blue, 1859–65 and disorderly; No. 31, the Bell Inn in 1736; No. 45, the Cross Keys in 1721; No. 49, the Swan (1855–1910). On the south side: No. 66, the Catherine Wheel in 1690; No. 68 or 73 (sources differ), White Hart (1776–1851); No. 79 (with the doorway in North Pallant), the Rifle or Rifleman (1854–1963); No. 80, the George (1604–64), but called the Anchor in 1573; and Nos 87–89, the Star (1537–97).

St Martin's Street in the north–east quadrant is linked to North Street by a twitten named The Crooked S, probably so called as this was once an area inhabited by pork butchers with their shambles (slaughterhouses). In St Martin's Street, to the north of this twitten, was the Trumpet Inn in 1697, which by 1755 was a house named the Old Trumpet. On the east side of St Martin's Street at No. 12 was the Kings Arms (1783–1903), and at 15a, the Black Horse Inn (1689–1730), now the site of a modern M&S store. The secluded south–east quadrant is characterised by affluent Georgian housing and offices and is also the site of Pallant House, the city art gallery. Lost inns of North Pallant were, on the east side, No. 5, Spread Eagle (1597–1682). On the west side at Nos 10–11 a house known in 1683 as the Globe may have been an inn; there was also, at Nos 18–20, Brewers Arms (1722–62). South Pallant was previously Plough Lane after the Plough Inn (1604–84) at Nos 18–19 on the west side at the West Pallant corner.

33. Waggon & Lamb, No. 34 Westgate (WG)

This Grade II-listed terraced house was the Mitre in 1780 and renamed by 1804. The nearby round Church of St Bartholomew had been destroyed during the Civil War and until its rebuilding in 1832 the business of the parish was conducted at this pub. An early landlord, Daniel Ide, died in 1833 aged seventy-two – a ripe old age for the time;

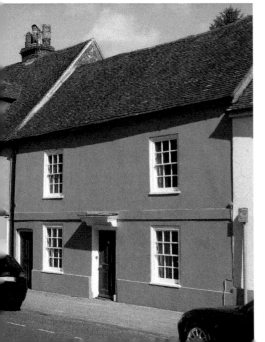

Waggon & Lamb.

however his father John had survived until 1823, just three days short of his 100th year. Upon this ceasing to be a pub in May 1939, landlord George William Davis, a retired naval lieutenant, had his licence transferred to the Crown Inn in Whyke Road.

34. Crate & Apple, Nos 12–14 Westgate (PBU-B)

This reopened in its present guise on 1 July 2015, having previously been the Vintage Pub & Bistro, and before that it was No. 12, but Cicestrians will remember it as the Swan. Its origins lie in a beerhouse of the 1850s. An early occupant was William Mant, who in 1861 was a brewer aged thirty-four employing one man and one boy. Brewing briefly resumed in the late 1870s with Walter Tart. The landlord of the early 1890s, Charles Aylmore, left to trade next door as a hairdresser. The Swan continued as a small beerhouse until 1936 when it was demolished by owners Portsmouth & Brighton United Breweries of Southsea, who erected the present premises. The planning application was not allowed to contravene the Restriction of Ribbon Development Act of 1935, legislation intended to prevent long strips of new housing along main roads leading out of population centres. One necessary concession was that the new building had to be at least 20 feet behind the front wall of the existing premises – the space has since been taken by the patio forecourt.

An intriguing feature of the proposed design was that the plans of 14 January 1936 by architect Stavers Hessell Tiltman show the aforementioned next door hairdressers also rebuilt and incorporated into the ground-floor area of the new premises, unmistakably placed behind the clearly drawn 20-foot 'improvement line' and positioned at the

Crate & Apple, originally the Swan.

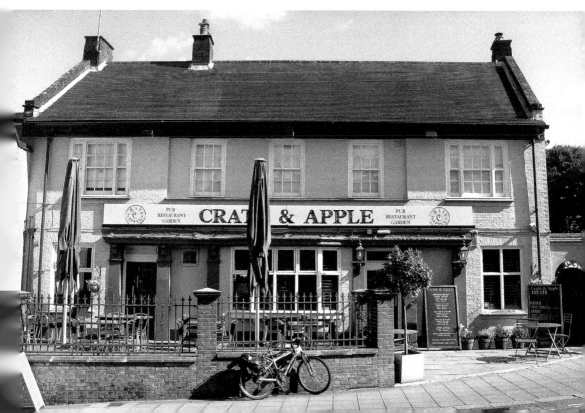

SWAN BREWERY,

WESTGATE, CHICHESTER.

WILLIAM MANT,

LICENSED

𝕭rewer and 𝕽etailer of 𝕭eer.

Families supplied with Small Casks at Wholesale Prices.

Superior Ales at 3d. 4d. & 5d. per Quart in your own Jugs.

AGENT FOR MEUX & CO'S. BROWN STOUT.

Swan advert, *Moore's Chichester Directory 1871.*

(still extant) far-left door and window. The now blocked-up partner door on that side originally gave access to a public bar; the existing door on the right led to a Bottle & Jug, while its now blocked-up partner was the entrance to the saloon bar; a games room was situated at the rear of a central servery. The fascia strip advertised United Ales and Stout. The rebuilding was no doubt prompted by the landlady at the time, Mrs Sarah Lale, having been referred for compensation in 1935 because of the house being structurally unfit and earmarked by the justices for redundancy. Sarah arrived with her husband Henry in 1907 and continued upon his death in 1914. She left in May 1947 and lived to be ninety-five.

35. Chichester Inn, No. 38 West Street (WG-F)

On a site once owned by the dean and chapter, this Grade II-listed eighteenth-century building was an inn named the Three Kings by 1754. Subsequently known as the Duke of Richmond or the Richmond Arms, it was the Castle by 1793. The site of Chichester Castle, a timber construction of the Norman period, stands some distance away to the north–east, so the name (if not generic) probably derives from the inn's former position by the castellated West Gate, which was demolished in 1773. The model for the castle depicted in the front window of what was once the bar parlour of the inn is clearly that at Windsor and was probably fitted during the interwar period.

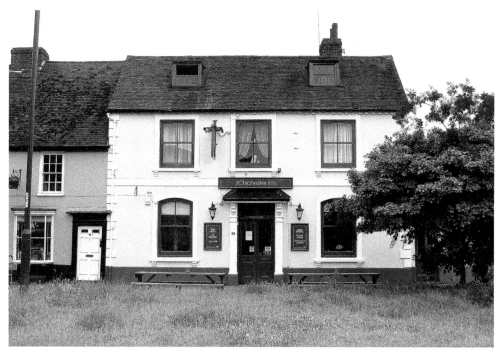

Above: Chichester Inn, formerly the Castle Inn.

Below: Chichester Inn front bar.

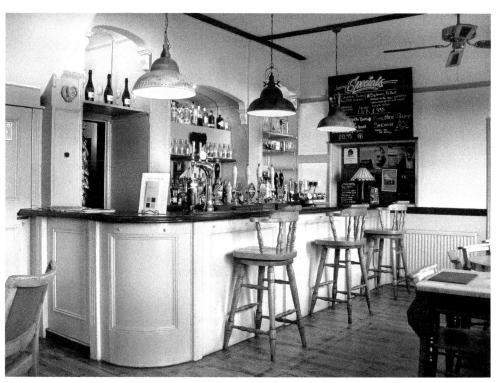

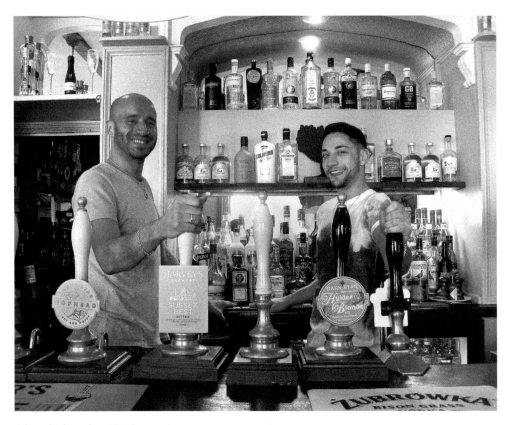

Al and El at the Chichester Inn.

The first known landlords were the Barrett family. In accordance with his wishes, Mr R. Barrett (landlord from 1804–08) was buried at the cathedral in the area within the cloisters known as Paradise. In November 1844, landlord James Heather hosted the Chichester Hand-Bell Club, which held its annual meeting here. The inn continued as the Castle until 10 October 1991 when it acquired its present name. A photograph of the front bar, with its interwar counter, appears on the cover of this book. Live acts appear on stage in the rear entertainments bar and the inn is currently home to the Chichester Folk Song Club. The ghost of a Roman centurion has been seen to pass through the pub, perhaps re-enacting his old route alongside the close by city walls. In 2005, the Sussex Paranormal Investigation Research Team (SPIRIT), attempted to detect paranormal activity at the inn as part of a fundraising charity event.

36. Red Lion, Nos 44–45 West Street (SS-WG)
This was the site of the Coopers Arms by 1784, rebuilt in 1816 by the Gatehouse family of the South Street Brewery and renamed the Red Lion. It closed as a pub _c._ 1900. Its precise position can be ascertained from its sign and roofline being visible in an 1897 photograph, although the present building is taller in comparison, possibly partially reconstructed.

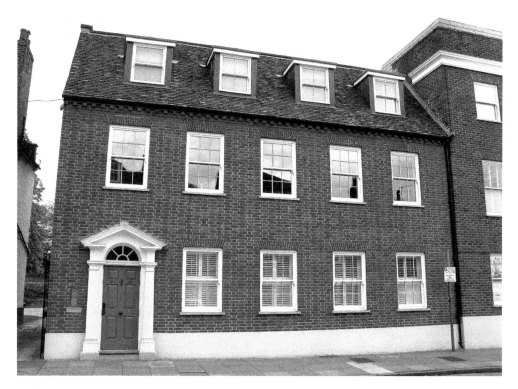

Red Lion.

37. Duke & Rye, No. 20 West Street

Turning a former house of worship into licensed premises is no longer a novel or particularly contentious idea, but the words sacrilege and desecration were freely banded about in letters to the local press after pub retailer Eldridge Pope and developers Spiremore Ltd announced a joint venture to convert the former Church of St Peter the Great into a bar called the Slurping Toad. The pub company did not help their cause by 'decorating' the interior with large plastic toads, while their attempt to honour the heritage of the building by altering its name to St Peter's Slurping Toad only further antagonised local feeling and, within two weeks of its opening on 29 October 1998, they were ordered to remove a mock pulpit. The developers had nonetheless negotiated and consulted with senior figures in the diocese over the project and had spent more than a million pounds engaging designer Tony Castley to sympathetically incorporate the original features of the church into a much-needed restoration, to the extent that they even employed the same stonemasons who had worked on the cathedral.

The church was built 1848–52 in the Gothic Revival style by Richard C. Carpenter, to a design described by architectural historian Nikolaus Pevsner as 'beautifully precise and sensitive'. The west porch of 1881 by Dunn & Hansom stands on the site of Carpenter's projected west tower. Virtually all the stained glass was blown out during the Second World War, and the east window depicting St Peter was installed in 1947. The Grade II-listed church was deconsecrated in 1982 and by 1998 was much

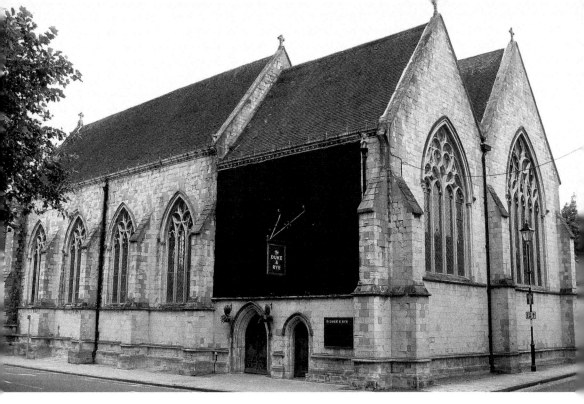

Above: Duke & Rye, originally the Slurping Toad.

Below: Preacher Man: President Trump at the Duke & Rye.

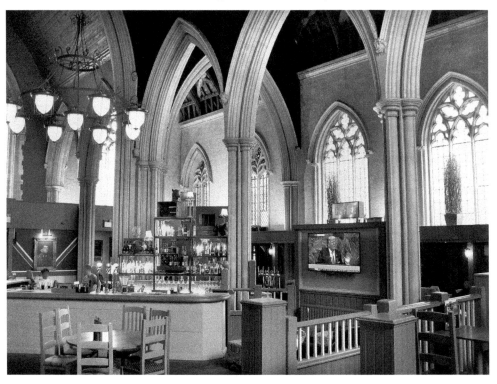

in need of repair. It had also seen previous commercial use as St Peter's Market and there appears not to have been any corresponding outpouring of outrage regarding this earlier retail function. After conversion to a bar, the Slurping part of the name was eventually dropped and in 2004, the Toad became West's Lounge & Bar. A further change occurred in 2016 with its acquisition by Marston's Brewery of Burton upon Trent and the adoption of its present name, which appears to refer to an obscure connection between the Duke of Wellington and the pub selling rye pale ale.

38. Prince of Wales, No. 1 Tower Street (EW-EA-F)

This Grade II-listed eighteenth-century building was a beerhouse by 1842. The premises then incorporated a bakehouse and William Etherton was a baker and beer retailer here from at least 1855–61. For two decades from 1890 George Charles Ancell ran the Prince of Wales in conjunction with a grocery. A past resident of the street recalled the story of his grandmother when a little girl was sent on an errand to Mr Ancell's shop for 1s 2d of vinegar. 'Sorry missie,' replied Mr Ancell, 'all my vinegar is sour', and so she returned home empty handed. The last licence renewal was in 1913. It was a printing works until 1996 and is now a private residence.

Prince of Wales.

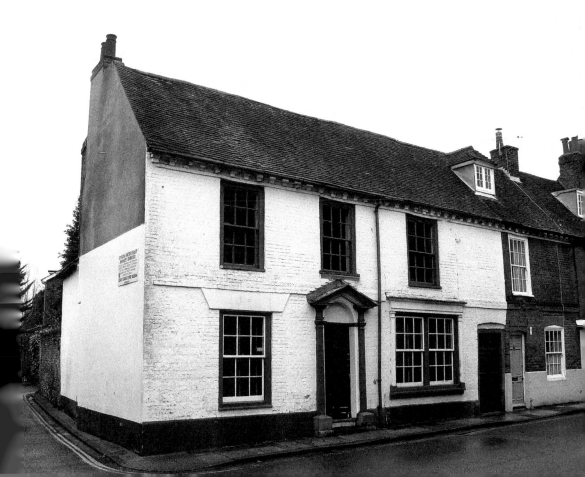

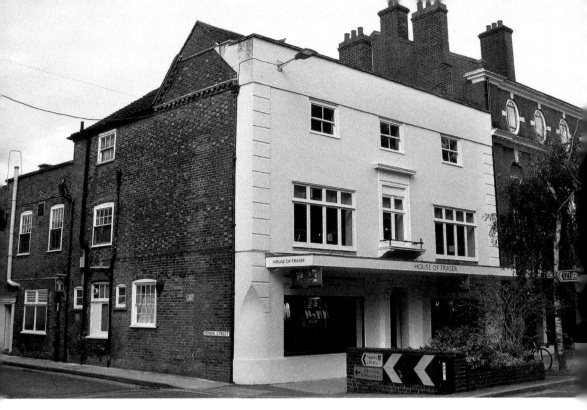

Eagle.

39. Eagle, No. 19 West Street (SS-WG)

On the corner with Tower Street and now incorporated into a department store, this was the Marquis of Granby Inn in 1798, renamed the Eagle by 1830 until 1903 when the licence was surrendered. It was a departing place for local carrier firms. The Ancient Order of Foresters (Court 'Constantia' No. 2206) held meetings here on the last Saturday of each month in 1890.

40. Belle Isle, Nos 31–32 Chapel Street

Part of a chain – the Belle Isle Company, which was established in 2010 – this particular outlet opened in a contemporary building in 2012. It advertises itself as a café-restaurant-bar – its post-modernism defying precise categorisation. The design concept invokes (in the overactive imagination of this author anyway) a glamorous cruise liner voyage to Buenos Aires in the 1920s. The decor is contemporary-retro. Or is it retro-contemporary? Having Googled both it seems there is a difference, although what it is remains unclear. Worn floorboards and matchwood bar counter, the latter ending in elegant deco curvature; rows of tea chests for storage; old enamelled tin advertisements for Oxo ('it's meat and drink to you'), Hammond's Chop Sauce ('hygienic Bakelite cap'). And yet nothing is as it first seems because the ambiance is so unmistakably 'here and now'. Materials are not simply reclaimed and upcycled but are carefully contrived to give the appearance of antiquity. The cans of baked beans, sacks of coffee beans and trays of Seville oranges are all faux, and there is an eccentric wall of old suitcases. The cases could not have been handpicked in

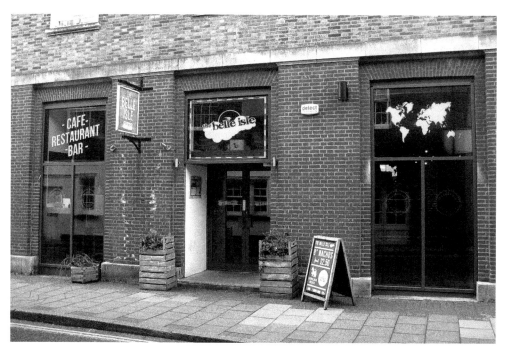

Above: Belle Isle exterior.

Below: Belle Isle interior.

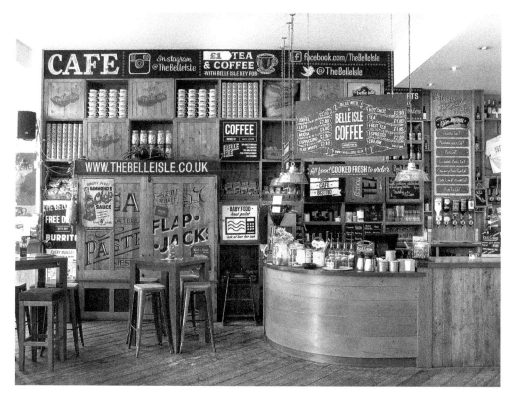

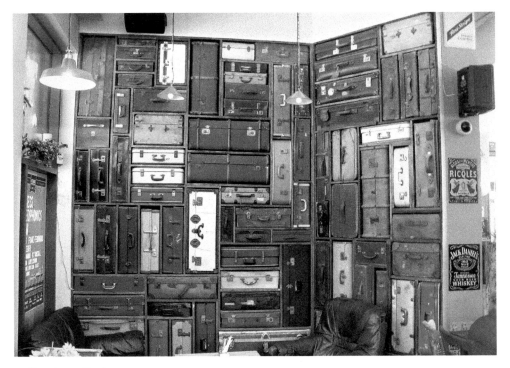

Belle Isle wall of suitcases.

their myriad sizes to exactly match the equally irregular shaped slots of the large wooden frame into which they all so snugly fit, so the whole caboodle must have been cleverly designed with the purpose in mind. The beer is also unmistakably contemporary and comes in both craft and cask form. The house offering on handpump is Sussex-brewed by Franklins. A 5.5 per cent IPA, it well compliments a tub of spicy nuts fresh from the jar on the bar, a perfect combo that is guaranteed to reinvigorate this author after a hard day mulling over dusty archives in the record office down the road.

41. Dolphin & Anchor, No. 9 West Street

This J D Wetherspoon outlet opened on 23 March 1999 with Jo Salter as manager. The first customers were Ben Hunt, Chris Hill and Gareth Wall. They ordered two Wetherspoon meals, one cheeseburger and three pints of Fosters, totalling £18 21p. On 23 July 2005 it became the first pub in the city to ban smoking on the premises. It was an £830,000 conversion of part of the former Dolphin & Anchor Hotel that had closed in 1997. On Wednesday 4 June of that year the hotel contents had been sold at auction in the first-floor ballroom. The last of the 658 lots was the sign hanging outside the front door. The buyers, a local family, later presented it to the city museum. The historic Grade II-listed hotel had itself been formed by a unification of two neighbouring but commercially warring and politically divided hostelries: the Dolphin (a Whig inn) and the Anchor (a Tory house). The present pub occupies what was the Anchor, while the larger site of the Dolphin has been converted to shops. Behind the eighteenth-century

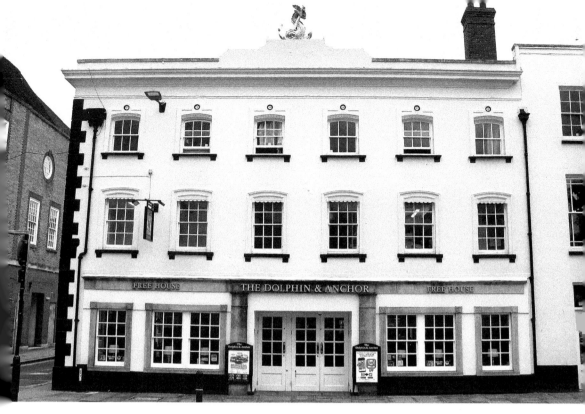

Above: Dolphin & Anchor: J D Wetherspoon.

Below: Anchor Hotel advert, *Moore's Chichester Directory 1880*.

THE ANCHOR

Family and Commercial Hotel,

WEST STREET, CHICHESTER.

Suites of Apartments.

COFFEE AND SMOKING ROOMS.

EDWARD BRAND,

Proprietor.

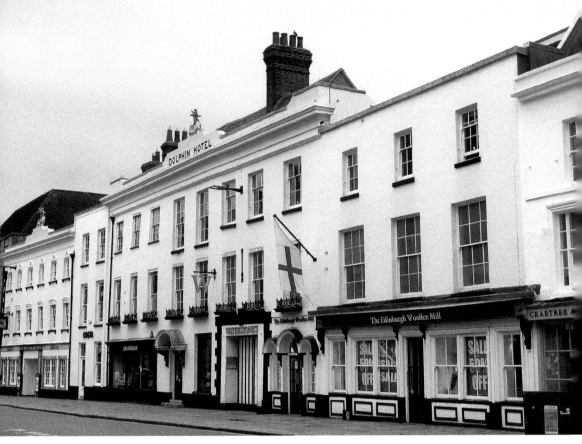

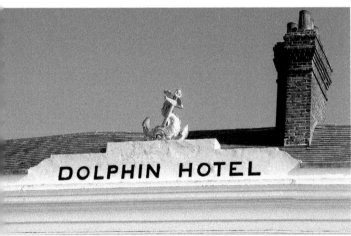

Above: Dolphin & Anchor Hotel.

Left: Dolphin Hotel parapet.

stuccoed frontage of the former hotel is an older brick building and there is documentary evidence of an earlier inn, the George (1486–1534), on or about the site of the Anchor.

The Anchor was known by 1671; it was the Blew (or Blue) Anchor in 1737, described in 1768 as 'new built' and called the Coal Exchange from 1807–28. During the time of William Combes, landlord from 1818–39, it housed a parrot that used to share its cage and food with a cat. Behind the grand coaching inn, separately accessed by a courtyard

BALLARD & SON,

Wine, Spirit, and Coal

MERCHANTS,

WEST STREET, CHICHESTER.

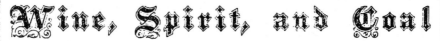

Good Dinner Sherry	.... 24/-, 27/- and 30/- per doz.	
Superior Sherries, pale or gold	.... 36/- to 54/-	,,
Good Ports	.... 24/-, 30/- and 36/-	,,
Superior ditto, crusted	.... 42/- to 84/-	,,
Light Dinner Clarets	.... 15/-, 18/-, 21/-, 24/- and 30/-	,,
Fine Clarets	.... 36/- to 84/-	,,

Choice Spirits of every description.

Bass and Allsopp's East India Pale Ales, Devenish and Co's. Celebrated Weymouth Dinner Ales, and London and Irish Stout, in Casks or Bottle.

Price Lists on Application.

DOLPHIN

Family and Commercial Hotel,

WEST STREET, CHICHESTER.

—o—

BALLARD AND SON, PROPRIETORS.

—o—

Open and closed Carriages and Post Horses for Hire.

HEARSE AND MOURNING COACHES.

Agents by Appointment to London, Brighton, and South Coast Railway Company, for supplying Carriages at the Station, and **Delivery of Goods and Parcels.**

Dolphin Hotel advert, *Moore's Chichester Directory 1883.*

was once a plebeian Anchor Tap. In 1818, it was the scene of a drunken disagreement between two soldiers – John Holloway and Thomas Parr – over who had earned the right to the company of Hannah Chase, a young woman who was free with her time with the men of the military in return for drinks and other such accruements. After punching Parr in the face, Holloway pursued him into what is now Chapel Street (then Upper West Lane), where he felled him by repeated musket blows to the back of the head, the fatal strike landing with such force that the butt of the weapon was detached from the stock. Convicted of murder, Holloway was hanged from an oak tree in the Gallows Field at the Broyle. His body was afterwards given to surgeons for dissection and then put on public display in the Council House before burial.

The first reference to the Dolphin is in 1649, although a stone bearing the date 1519 was once discovered in a chimney during renovations. The inn was described in 1794 as 'new built'. It originally consisted of the central portion of eight bays, where its name is still etched on the parapet, later extended to both the east (three bays) and west (two bays). To the right of the hooded doorway with fanlights is the square entrance to what was the old mews with its stabling. It was here in the hayloft that post-chaise driver Richard Pulter hanged himself in March 1763. Another driver of the inn, Reuben Benham, was drowned one rainy, windswept night in January 1808, his chaise plunging into the wharf at nearby Midhurst after he misjudged the road over the bridge. His great-grandson (long yet to be born) would be the writer H. G. Wells. In March 1813, landlord Charles Triggs collapsed and died in his bar parlour, aged just twenty-seven and only three months after his welcoming party. William Ballard was landlord from 1832–68. His wife Maria was the last person in the city to travel by sedan chair, and their son Adolphus (eventual owner of the Dolphin) was to become Mayor of Chichester in 1896–97.

By that period, both inns were facing the future and advertising themselves as 'Family and Commercial Hotels'. Yet they were to forego their family proprietorship. An entry of 6 April 1907 in the local licensing register records the Anchor coming under ownership of the Sussex Public House Trust Co Ltd. This was a regional body of the Central Public House Trust Association, formed in 1901 with the aim of public house reform. It was modelled on the Gothenburg system of 'disinterested management' with pubs run by salaried managers who took no profits on liquor sales so felt no pressure to 'push the trade' and promote drunkenness. The Sussex scion became 'Home Counties' in 1911 and Trust Houses Limited in 1919, who on 17 May that year were first recorded in the licensing register as owners of the Dolphin. The two hotels still had separate licences in 1921 but were issued for the first time to the same manager. The phrase 'Dolphin & Anchor' first appears in the licensing register on 4 February 1922, along with 'altered to one licence'. The hotel was thus born of the same impetus that gave rise to the 'improved public house movement' of the interwar era. Through a merger in 1970, the company became Trust Houses Forte.

The Licensees
Ernest John Lough, acting secretary of the Sussex Public House Trust Company, the new owners of the Anchor, became the licence holder of the hotel in May 1907. The company offices were in London so his authority was likely nominal. He was born in

Peckham in October 1872 and married Minnie Blaxill in June 1896. In 1901, he was a chartered accountant's clerk in Enfield. By 1911 he was no longer license holder of the Anchor and was living in Brighton, where Millie died in October 1912. The following month Ernest was initiated into the Adur Lodge of the Brighton Freemasons, his profession given as accountant. He remarried Charlotte Bravington in 1914, who died in 1928. Ernest dies in March 1933 in West Ham.

Alexander Francis Part (1876–1955) was educated at Harrow and Trinity College Cambridge, after which he practised as a barrister until called to the bar in a different profession as co-manager of the Hertfordshire Public House Trust Company. Part became licence holder of the Anchor from 1912–13 as MD of the Home Counties Public Trust House, then licence holder of the Dolphin from 1919–21 until his resignation as MD of Trust Houses Limited. The following year saw the publication of his book, *The Art and Practice of Innkeeping*.

42. Royal Arms, No. 92 East Street (C-WG-T)

Behind the post-1715 Georgian stucco and bow windows of this Grade II*-listed building is a sixteenth-century timber-framed construction with overhanging upper floors. Originally two wings, the eastern half was once the parsonage of St Mary's Church. In 1591, the site was the townhouse of courtier and statesman Lord John Lumley. Tradition has it that in August of that year, as an aspect of Her Majesty's Royal Progress in West Sussex and Hampshire, Lumley entertained Elizabeth I in the first-floor front room, subsequently

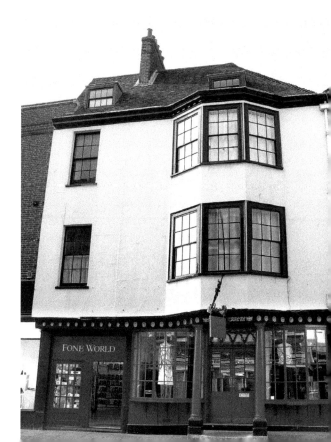

Royal Arms, aka the Punch House.

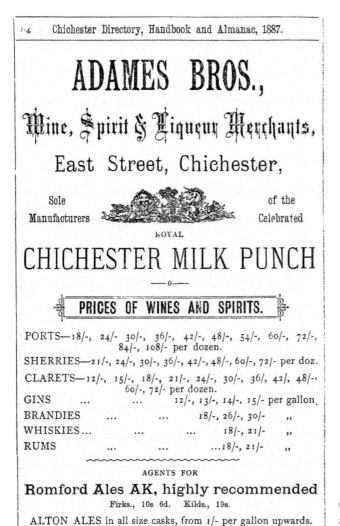

ADAMES BROS.,

𝔚𝔦𝔫𝔢, 𝔖𝔭𝔦𝔯𝔦𝔱 & 𝔏𝔦𝔮𝔲𝔢𝔲𝔯 𝔐𝔢𝔯𝔠𝔥𝔞𝔫𝔱𝔰,

East Street, Chichester,

Sole Manufacturers · · · of the Celebrated

ROYAL

CHICHESTER MILK PUNCH

PRICES OF WINES AND SPIRITS.

PORTS—18/-, 24/- 30/-, 36/-, 42/-, 48/-, 54/-, 60/-, 72/-, 84/-, 108/- per dozen.

SHERRIES—21/-, 24/-, 30/-, 36/-, 42/-, 48/-, 60/-, 72/- per doz.

CLARETS—12/-, 15/-, 18/-, 21/-, 24/-, 30/-, 36/, 42/, 48/-, 60/-, 72/- per dozen.

GINS ... ... 12/-, 13/-, 14/-, 15/- per gallon.

BRANDIES ... ... 18/-, 26/-, 30/- ,,

WHISKIES... ... ... 18/-, 21/- ,,

RUMS ... ...18/-, 21/- ,,

AGENTS FOR

Romford Ales AK, highly recommended

Firks., 10s 6d.   Kilds., 19s.

ALTON ALES in all size casks, from 1/- per gallon upwards.

Chichester Milk Punch advert, *Moore's Chichester Directory 1887.*

known as the Audience Room or Elizabethan Room; its exceptional moulded plaster ceiling of that period is thought to have been the work of Italian craftsmen. A descendant of Lumley was created Earl of Scarborough in 1690 and the property was for some years afterwards called Scarborough House (or Mansion). At what point it became an inn is uncertain but part of the ground floor was converted to a shop c. 1800.

The Royal Arms, as the inn was titled, became known informally as the Punch House after a powerful concoction called Chichester Milk Punch. This liqueur was first attributed to one E. Parker, a Georgian wine merchant in the undercroft of the Vicars' Hall; his trade card announced him as 'Manufacturer of Milk Punch to His Majesty'. By around 1832, John Hudson, probably the same man as had been landlord of the Dolphin in West Street, was at the Royal Arms and in 1840 was granted a royal charter by Queen Victoria commanding him to the place of 'Manufacturer of Milk

Punch in Ordinary to Her Majesty'. From 1855 through to the first decade of the twentieth century, the Royal Arms traded as a wine, spirits and liqueur merchants, whose successive owners and licensees, most notably the Adames family, advertised themselves as 'Sole Manufacturers of the Celebrated Royal Chichester Milk Punch'.

In 1926, owners Henty & Constable of the Westgate Brewery made alterations to create the Oak Lounge with genuine old panelling taken from the Elizabethan Room. The leaded windows of the lounge bore the coats of arms of Tudor monarchs. From here could be viewed a walled garden in which some Roman coins were once unearthed. It was during these renovations that an oak beam was uncovered bearing the date 1595 and the name William Holland, founder of Steyning Grammar School and thrice Mayor of Chichester from 1580. On display in the lounge was a huge cask of the kind once used to store milk punch. When the queen visited the city in 1987, she was presented by the pub landlord, Dennis Pordage, with a bottle of punch that he had produced from the original recipe. In 2006, six years after the pub had suffered a serious fire, it was closed and converted into retail outlets and private apartments.

The Landlords
Wine and Spirit Merchant George Adames was at the Royal Arms by 1870. He died aged about fifty-three on 2 December 1879, his wife Augusta surviving him only until 6 March 1881 and short of her fiftieth year. Their sons, Thomas Bridger and Frederick (Fred) James then ran the business as the Adames Brothers until 1891 when Thomas left to take over the Anchor in West Street. Thomas died aged thirty-eight on 23 December 1896, leaving his wife Jane as licensee of the Anchor until 1899. Fred continued at the Royal Arms until his death aged thirty-nine on 12 December 1900. His wife Ina Emily carried on the licence until her own death, aged forty-three on 26 January 1906.

43. Hole in the Wall, No. 1a St Martin's Street (B)
A plaque in the north porch entrance of this pub claims that the original building is believed to have been a debtors' prison and that the name comes from a hole made in the wall to enable visitors to pass food to the convicts. No documentary evidence has been found of such a former usage, and a highly reliable source states that this was a newly built malthouse and dwelling in 1746. This date near enough coincides with the inscription of 1742 on a large stone in the current bar area. There was once a poorhouse (workhouse) a few doors away so it is possible that food was passed to inmates there though a wall. A more plausible suggestion is that the name arose because such a hole was made so that beer could be passed to a man working in the stores of the St Martin's Brewery, which this site was from at least 1785 until 1883. It was afterwards the St Martin's Brewery Inn. William John Parsons was landlord from 1915–27. His directory listing for his departing year reads: 'wine & spirit vaults; fully licensed caterer; good accommodation for parties; large tea garden.' The change of name to the Hole in the Wall did not occur until a May 1951 request from owners Brickwoods Brewery. In 1954, the Royal Antediluvian Order of Buffaloes (Regnum Lodge No. 959) convened here on Wednesdays. At the end of 1961 the Chichester Folk Song and Dance Club was formed and first met weekly on Fridays at the pub.

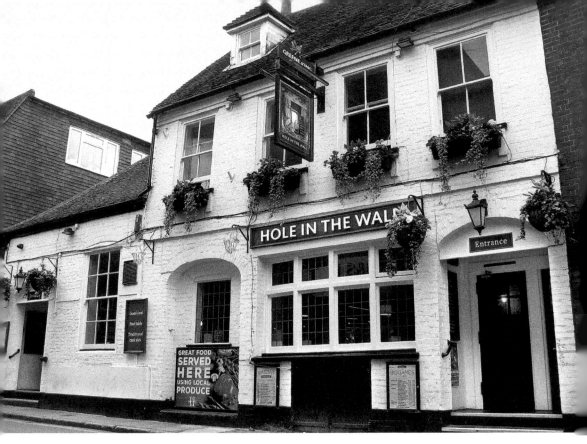

Hole in the Wall, formerly the St Martin's Brewery Inn.

44. Crab & Lobster, No. 12 St Martin's Square (EW)

William McMaster was a tea dealer here in 1841 and within a few years was also running a beershop. He was succeeded by his son John Woods McMaster, a tailor by trade. In 1860, he was fined for refusing a policeman entry to the house. The licence was not renewed after September 1888. Nos 11–12 form a Grade II-listed pair.

45. Curriers Arms, No. 11 Little London (EW-EA-F)

The private house named Curriers is the left of a pair of properties known by 1788 and now Grade II listed. A currier worked on hides of leather after tanning, a trade that in the seventeenth century was concentrated in the East Street area of the city. One of three beer retailers in Little London in 1839 could have been operating from here, but by 1851 this was a bakers and beer retailers under the partnership of Susannah Boniface and her younger widowed sister Frances Pannell. A valuation of 1867 records the ground-floor premises to consist of a front shop with entrance, back sitting room, scullery, flour store and bakehouse. The Miles family took over operations from 1882 until 1921 when the licence for the nearby Prince Arthur was renewed on the understanding that the owning brewery of both houses – Friary, Holroyd & Healy – would not oppose the police objection to the renewal of the licence for the Curriers Arms. The Miles family continued on the premises as grocers with the Lass brothers as bakers.

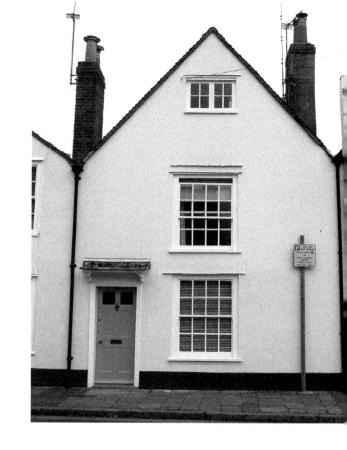

Right: Crab & Lobster.

Below: Curriers Arms.

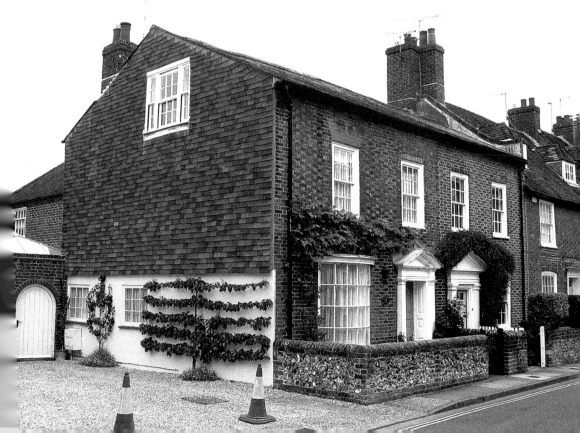

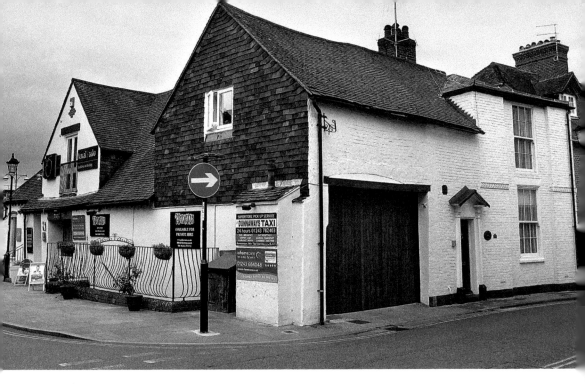

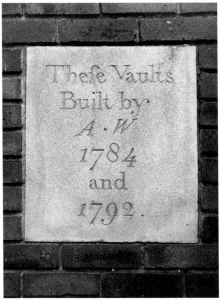

Above: Golden Cross and site of Jackson's Cellar.

Left: Plaque above Golden Cross vault.

46. Golden Cross, Nos 2–2a Little London (SS-WG)

On premises previously a malthouse and stables and in 1716 a religious meeting house, by 1750 this was the King of Prussia and renamed the Golden Cross in 1829 under new landlord John Battcock. In the early nineteenth century, carrier wagons left here three days a week for Pulborough, Portsmouth and Southampton. In 1849, landlord James Guy was severely admonished for keeping late hours, while a brief incumbent of 1852, Robert Cobden, was cautioned as to the conduct of his house. The license was surrendered in 1903 and the premises are now Golden Cross House – part residential, part commercial. As more than a postscript: in 1985, the Noble Rot restaurant and wine bar was set up in the vault of the old inn, to be succeeded a decade later by Jackson's Cellar. Run by Cicestrian beer enthusiast Roger Jackson, this cosy free house sold a range of real ales plus draught and bottled Belgian beers, closing *c.* 1998. A recently refaced stone above the steps notes the vault to have been built by A. W. in 1784 and 1792. The initials stand for Alexander Williams.

47. Prince Arthur, No. 41 Little London (EW-EA-F)

This Grade II-listed building of the eighteenth century or earlier could have been the site of the Victoria, known in 1844–45 under William Ginman. It was the Masons Arms by 1861 under stonemason and beerhouse keeper John Gutterson and was probably renamed (after Queen Victoria's third son) soon afterwards under John Earwaker, also a grocer and bricklayer. Sergeant Harry William Beacher (1864–1962) of the West Sussex Constabulary once lodged here disguised as a coachman in an attempt to apprehend some gamblers. This was the last remaining beerhouse in Chichester, a publican's licence finally being granted in February 1954 to George Walter Holland, who had taken over two years previously. He had retired from the army in 1946 with the rank of lieutenant colonel after thirty-eight years' service. The pub at that time had a private bar and very large public bar; it ran a Tontine Club with sixty members and had a darts club of forty members. The licence was surrendered in May 1980 after the arrival the previous November of Friary Meux house-manager Peter Street. The premises are now in retail use.

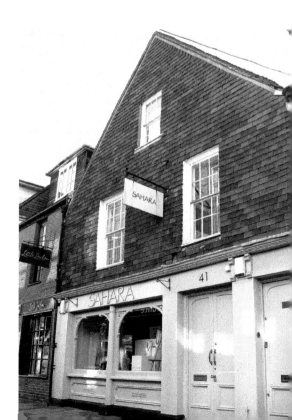

Prince Arthur.

48. Fleece, No. 58 East Street (WG-F)

The wrought-iron bracket of the sign remains as a reminder of the pub at No. 58, while the position of the triangular pediment indicates the much larger inn that once extended westward to encompass Nos 59–60, with all three properties now Grade II listed. An alehouse was here in 1641. It was the Coach & Horses or the Coach Inn by 1710 and was refronted five years later when the underhang of the jetty was bricked up. It became the Bell from 1724 until September 1794, when it was refurbished under new landlord John Battcock and renamed the Golden Fleece. In 1819, landlord Richard Hewlins enlarged the premises through acquisition of the adjoining private house to provide extra accommodation. From the mid-nineteenth century it became known simply as the Fleece. The Good Intent Friendly Society and the Ancient Order of Foresters (Court 'Prince of Wales', No. 4879) both met here in 1909.

The oak beams of the old timber-framed building were a noted feature of the three-bar interior – saloon, lounge and public – in a pub guide of 1966. John Brierley, landlord from 1951–66, was also a mechanic and a gifted amateur photographer of the motor racing scene. Brierley helped Stirling Moss jack up and repair his Lotus Elite after the driver had damaged the car reversing out of the inn yard on the April 1962 morning of the Goodwood crash that ended Moss's professional racing career. In September 1965, owning brewery, Friary Meux had applied unsuccessfully for a change of use to a retail shop. When the Fleece closed in 1988 the Major of Chichester, Martin French, put forward an ambitious plan to convert the premises into a non-alcoholic bar for teenagers, but the wishes of Friary Meux prevailed and the Fleece finally became a shop twenty-five years after the first asking.

Fleece.

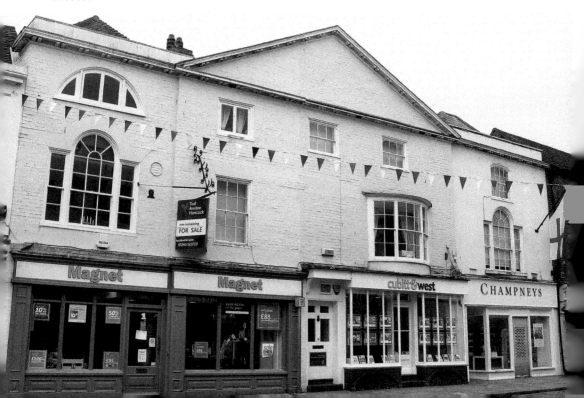

4

Beyond the East Walls

Our fourth and final walk commences in Eastgate Square, which was rebuilt after being completely laid to waste in the Civil War. Two of the buildings destroyed were the following inns: in the middle of what is now the open centre of the square was the Dolphin in 1632; on the north side at No. 1 was the Lion in 1604. The Running Horse beerhouse was at No. 3 from 1839–1903, after which it became a fried fish shop; the site has since been replaced by the modern block of buildings before the parish church. A venison feast took place in November 1822 at the Barge Inn, its location in the square remains unknown, as does that of the Eastgate Lunch House under beer retailer William Willis in 1858.

We now walk north–east past the church into St Pancras. A street on the south–east side called the Needlemakers is after one of the many artisan industries carried on centuries ago in this once impoverished and plague-ridden suburb. On this same side at No. 145 and opposite New Park Road was the Plough & Harrow from 1795–1914, but called the Chequers in 1785. The building was redeveloped and extended in 1939 as an office and showroom. Four doors west of No. 89 was the Black Boy in 1627, which closed by 1807. On the north–east side at No. 34 was the Hope from 1837–1931 and subsequently was demolished. Richard Urry was a beer retailer and millwright at No. 58 in 1855–59, which is now approximately the site of Adelaide Road.

We now turn right down St James Road, this area being Portfield, after the large common field once here. At Nos 19–22 (formerly Bottle Lane) was the Leather (or Leathern) Bottle in 1831, renamed the Bricklayers Arms in 1833 and demolished two years after becoming a private residence in 1857. We then come to Oving Road, where at No. 203 was the Chequers from 1861–2012, which closed following a fire and demolished in 2013 for new houses. We now make a short detour south to pubs at Bognor Road and Whyke Road. A lost pub at the junction of these roads was the Roundabout House in 1841–1935. Retracing our steps and heading west we eventually enter the Hornet where at an unknown location Thomas Carver ran the Live and Let Live in 1845–55.

49. Market Tavern, No. 16 Eastgate Square (R)

Newly built in 1813, this was a beerhouse by 1855 under tailor John Richard Hammond. His widow Frances continued the licence for three years until 1888. The name Market Tavern first appears following the opening of the nearby Cattle Market on 10 May 1871. The tavern was owned by the Rock Brewery of Brighton when it closed in 1925 and the licence was transferred to the Nags Head in St Pancras. The Grade II-listed building is now in retail use but the tavern name remains in old ceramic tiles behind the modern fascia and is periodically revealed whenever owners renew their signboard.

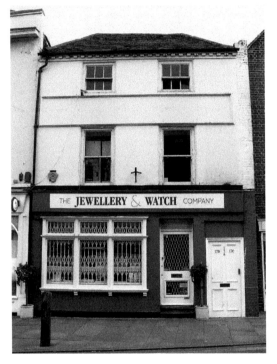

Left: Market Tavern.

Below: Market Tavern advert, *Moore's Chichester Directory 1883*.

---

28   **Chichester Directory, Handbook and Almanac, 1883.**

JOHN RICHARD HAMMOND,

Market Tavern,

EAST GATE, CHICHESTER,

——o——

SUPERIOR ALES, WINES AND SPIRITS.

Tailor, &c.

50. Cattle Market Inn, No. 13 Eastgate Square

This Grade II-listed building of *c.* 1811 stands on the site of an earlier malthouse and mill-house. It was known by 1867 and until 1871 as the Devonshire Inn under landlord James Stevens but may have existed earlier as a beerhouse. It was owned from 1872 by a succession of small, local brewers until purchased in 1920 by lessee Gale's who closed and sold it in 1988 for conversion to retail use. A 1974 pub guide described the interior as one bar stretched around the L-shaped building with a separate twelve-seat grill room. Laura, the resident parrot, was said to have been around 140 years old – the same age as the inn.

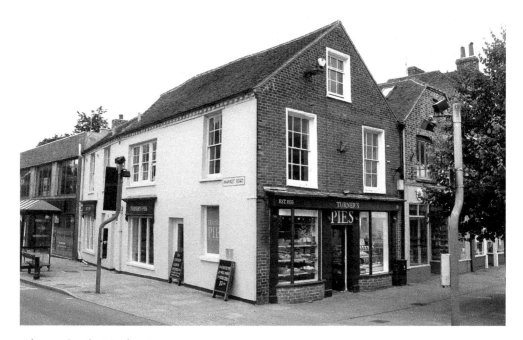

Above: Cattle Market Inn.

Below: Cattle Market Inn advert, *Moore's Chichester Directory 1880*.

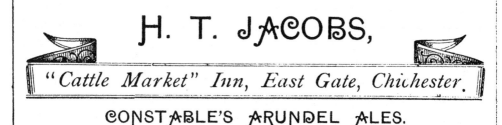

51. Bull Inn, Nos 4–5 Market Road (EW-EA-F)

The earliest known reference to this pub is from December 1871, which suggests that it began trading upon the opening of the Cattle Market opposite. The first landlord was John William Vick, here until February 1873. His name was discovered under several layers of paint during alterations of 1956. During the First World War, landlord George Linkhorn billeted officers from the 9th Hampshire Cycling Division who were passing through on their way to fight in France. One of George's regulars was local thatcher Jack Green. On seeing Jack set foot in the door George would immediately pull him two pints. Jack would gulp down the first in one go before supping the second more slowly. In 2002, this hitherto traditional market traders' pub was gutted and 'themed' as a young person's venue with bouncers on the door. Two years later under Chinese owners it became the White Tiger. Following another extensive refurbishment, it reopened as the Bull in 2007 under Jamie Boyle, previously of the Four Chesnuts in Oving Road. In 2010, it was taken by Keith Dixon and Bill O'Hagan on a five-year free-of-tie lease and became renowned for its real ale and sausages. It closed in 2015 and remains in disuse.

52. Unicorn Inn, No. 8 Eastgate Square (WG-T)

The inn was in existence by 1670 and the Corporation of St Pancras was founded here in 1689, a mock corporate body of eminent townsfolk that elected various officers, including a mayor. Afterwards a purely charitable organisation, it originally celebrated the overthrow of the Catholic James II and the accession to the throne of the Protestant William III and Mary II. The Corporation acquired the nickname of the Wheelbarrow Club after the means by which apprentices conveyed home their drunken

Bull Inn.

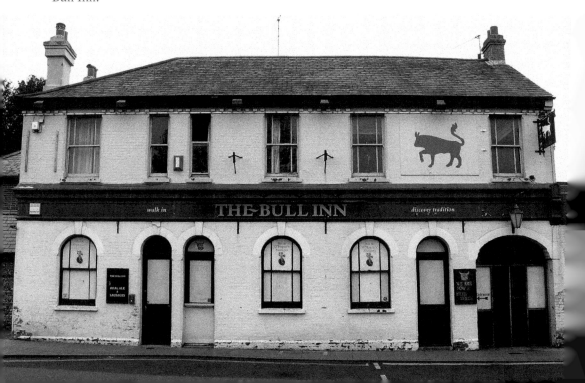

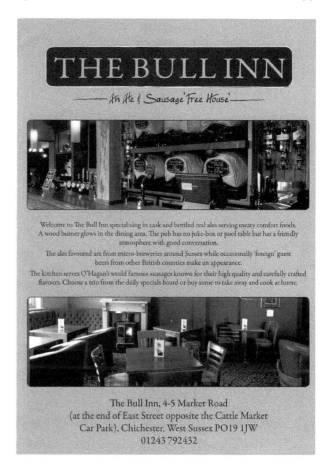

Bull Inn flyer (author's collection).

masters following the feasts held at the Unicorn every 4 November, King William's birthday. The inn was largely rebuilt in 1760. Over a century later, the city still lacked a sewerage system, its insantiary streets being a source of disease, yet objections to proposed remedies continued to be raised on the grounds of expense. In October 1889, the self-styled Anti-Drainage Party met here and offered the following peculiar, but to them probably impeccable piece of logic: 'a bucket of urine thrown on the ground would spread itself over the ground, be dried up by the sun, and in a short time there would be nothing to see or smell'. A very different form of self-help organisation that met here, in 1909, was the Ancient Order of Foresters (Court 'Constantia', No. 2206).

To plans dated 10 October 1938, the inn was demolished and rebuilt further back from the old site. It was formally reopened with a dinner in 1941. During the Second World War, the small upstairs bar was known as the Heroes Room, its walls hung with signed photographs of RAF squadrons. Among the pilots of the nearby fighter base of Tangmere who used to frequent the bar was renowned ace Douglas Bader. The infamous cut of cards to decide whether Friary or Tamplins had first choice of the barrelage-ranked Henty & Constable tied estate of pubs took place here in 1955. Lunch was provided by landlord Doug Harcourt, ex-Fleet Air Arm Petty Officer, RAF Squadron Leader and

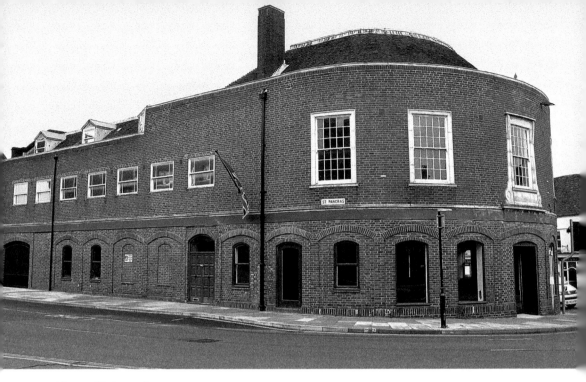

Above: Unicorn Inn.

Below: Unicorn Inn advert, *Moore's Chichester Directory 1887*.

---

44   Chichester Directory, Handbook and Almanac, 1887.

THOMAS LEE,

Unicorn Inn,

EAST GATE, CHICHESTER.

———o———

Good Bed and Sitting Rooms.   Good Stabling and Lock-up Coach Houses.

Wines and Spirits of the Best Quality.

---

holder of the Distinguished Flying Cross. He was at the Unicorn from 1951 until its closure in 1960. Proposals to turn the pub into offices and showrooms or a petrol station with a garage were rejected and in 1962 it became the Minerva Studios, costumers of the Chichester Festival Theatre. It was afterwards newspaper offices and currently stands vacant but is earmarked for retail use. Now called Unicorn House, the Chichester City Council Blue Plaque celebrating its heritage as an inn was installed in 2015.

53. Nags Head, No. 3 St Pancras (R-PBU-B)

This imposing mock-Tudor pub has its origins in the Horses Head, a small beershop with a forge at the rear. Joseph Bridger was blacksmith and beer retailer here in 1851. Subsequent occupants carried on both trades until 1915. It was owned by the local Walberton Brewery before being acquired at auction in 1922 by the Red Lion Brewery of Hoare & Co. Ltd, East London, who rebuilt the house in its present half-timbered form. Plans by architect F. O. Marchant dated June 1923 were approved in October 1924 and the work probably completed the following year, as in March 1925 a full licence was obtained via a transfer from the closed Market Tavern in Eastgate Square. The prominent jettied and gabled central bay originally accessed a Jug & Bottle to the left and a private bar to the right. A covered walkway at the far left marked the old entrance to the forge. The door at this side led to a public bar. The doorway at the far right gave entrance to the market dining room. A hall and a parlour lay to the rear of the central servery. Alterations and additions to the premises, including the erection of a rear dining room were carried out by Portsmouth & Brighton United Breweries in the late 1930s and the pub has more recently been subject to refurbishment and renovation. The east extension received a 2001 Chichester City Council Heritage Blue Plaque Award. In 2005, some internal walls were removed and a conservatory extension installed.

54. Black Horse, Nos 141–142 St Pancras (EA)

This Grade II-listed property dates from *c.* 1798 and was the freehold of the Custos of St Mary's Hospital. It was occupied in 1821 by victualler and ex-cordwainer

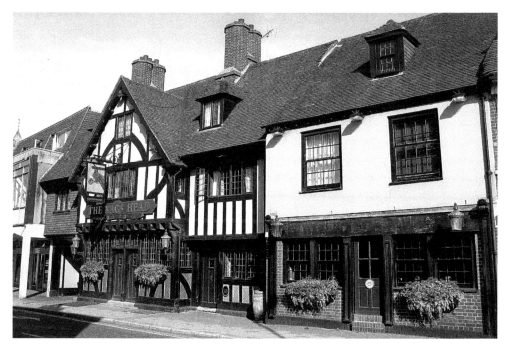

Nags Head, rebuilt 1925.

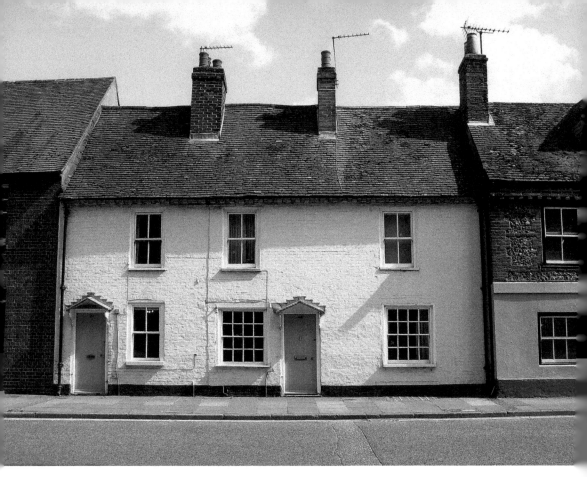

Black Horse.

George Winsor. By 1840 it was known as the Black Horse beerhouse under landlord Joseph Dawtry. In 1843, John Sutcliffe was committed for trial for the theft of a coat and trousers from Dawtry. The landlord of 1861, Joseph Thrift, was fined for selling beer after 11 p.m. After the loss of the license in 1890, landlady Lucy Baughan continued to run the premises as a lodging house.

55. Victoria, No. 25 St Pancras (C-WG-T)

After a previous refusal of the licence application, this became a pub in 1850 under the Deller family, owners until 1894 and who also had the older brewery at the rear. When international motor race meetings were held at Goodwood during the 1950s, the Ferrari mechanics would stay here and be entertained by a talking bird in a cage. In 1969, this was one of a number of pubs in the city for which the application by Tamplins (part of Watney Mann) for an illuminated Red Barrel sign was refused by the council as 'seriously detrimental' to the character of the area. The pub was sold the following year and became a free house after having its Victorian interior gutted. During the 1980s it gained a reputation as a music venue, during which time the cellars and long-redundant brewhouse were converted to a restaurant. The pub closed in late 1989 and became offices.

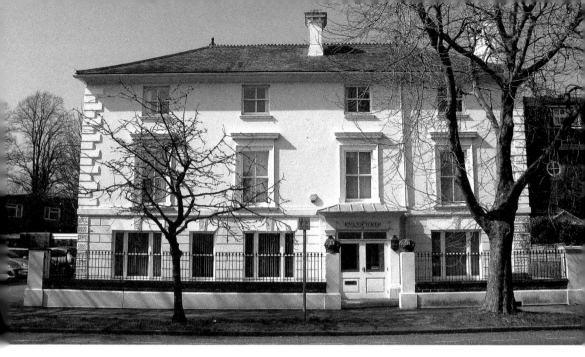

Victoria.

56. Coach & Horses, No. 125c St Pancras (WG-T)

Shortly before 5 p.m. on a Saturday in December 2003, landlord Colin McAndrew and teacher Richard Marsden saw the spectral figure of a woman move speedily from the front of this pub through the bar to disappear at the rear. She had long, dark hair, was clad in long, grey sackcloth or hessian, tied at the middle by a cord, and was carrying a bundle. This sighting was accompanied by a distinct breeze and rapid drop in temperature. The pub dog leapt to the opposite side of the room, its ears down, whimpering. It would not return to its previous spot for two days. An expert in the paranormal thought the woman to have been a victim of the plague epidemic of the seventeenth century.

Formerly the Angel Inn and known from 1754, this became the Coach & Horses between 1805 and 1811. In 1849, John MacGillicaddy was fined for malicious damage to a bedroom door here. Four years later, John Paynter was charged with stealing a copper pot to the value of 2s, the property of landlord John Reynolds. A long-serving landlord of the twentieth century was Fred Pullen, here with his wife Amy for nearly twenty-five years from 1947. They died within a month of each other at a nursing home in 1993, aged ninety-four and ninety-three, respectively.

Two years after the pub was purchased in 1996 by King & Barnes of Horsham, that brewery's mild won landlord Colin Clarke the Midhurst, Chichester & Bognor CAMRA branch Mild Trophy, awarded to the pub that offered the best all-year-round mild ale. In 2000, King & Barnes and its pubs were acquired by Hall & Woodhouse, who ten years later closed and sold the Coach & Horses for conversion to private accommodation. The signboard remains, although somewhat faded by now, and the paint-over that obliterated the name of the brewery is beginning to peel.

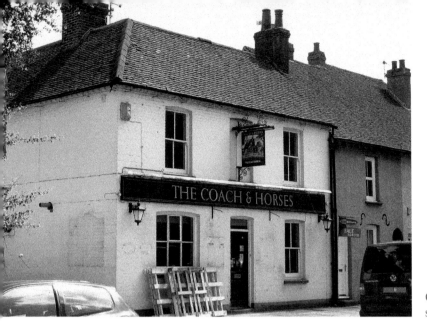

Coach & Horses
soon after closing.

57. Ship & Lighter, No. 118 St Pancras (WG)

This Grade II-listed building has a date stone of 1700, above which is a complicated monogram that appears to be 'E R' entwined with its mirror image. It was an inn by 1797 under landlord John Clear. Downstairs was a large room with flagstone floor and open fireplace, enclosed each side by a high-backed settle. Upstairs was a long clubroom for dinners and functions. Here, in November 1815, William Huskisson, MP for Chichester, entertained a party of friends. Fifteen years later, he was the first person to die in a railway accident, having fallen under Stephenson's Rocket at the opening of the Liverpool to Manchester line. The venison feasts held upstairs each November in the 1820s were in Protestant celebration of 'The Glorious Revolution of 1688', and in the following decade a Corporation of St Pancras was formed here as a short-lived alternative to the established club of that name at the Unicorn Inn in Eastgate Square.

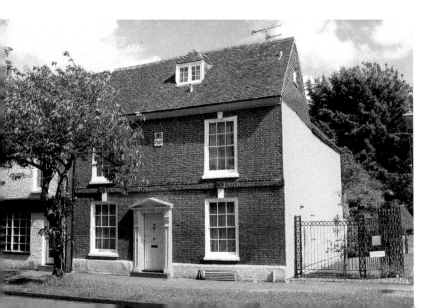

Ship & Lighter.

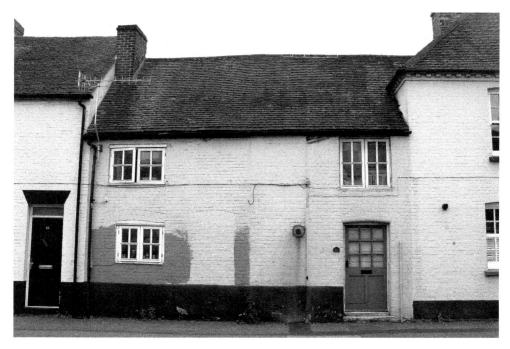

Star & Garter.

For a period in 1856, landlord James Broad had his licence refused for preventing entry to a policeman in search of a man who had stolen a watch. The license was surrendered in 1903 and the premises continued as a lodging house under landlady Emma Langley.

58. Star & Garter, No. 89 St Pancras (WG-F)
This was first named in 1801 and had been leased to a brewer in 1785. It was also a lodging house with nine boarders recorded in the 1851 census and eighteen in 1861. The landlord from 1841–51, Robert Smart, was a stonemason who died in his forties. James Shippam, landlord from 1853–87, was fined on two occasions in 1864: the first for having 'unjust' measures, the second for opening before 12.30 p.m. on a Sunday. The landlord of 1957–59 was bestowed with the magnificent name of Roydon Percy James Hamilton Hall. Perhaps he was simply known as Roy. It was said that when Friary Meux manager Peter Street took over a pub it was a sure sign of its impending closure, and so it was when he arrived here in March 1980 with the license surrendered six months later.

59. Red Lion, No. 78 St Pancras (EA-F)
Also serving as a lodging house, this was first named in 1839 under landlord Henry Sopp but was probably the same pub as the Golden Lion, known from 1832–39 and run by the Florance family who owned the Lion Brewery and lived nearby at Lion House. The landlord of 1881, Charles Ide, was a blacksmith who moved the following year to the Barley Mow in Oving Road. Harry Burchett, landlord 1891–94, was also a fried fish merchant, a foretelling of the pub's eventual fate after it closed *c.* 1984.

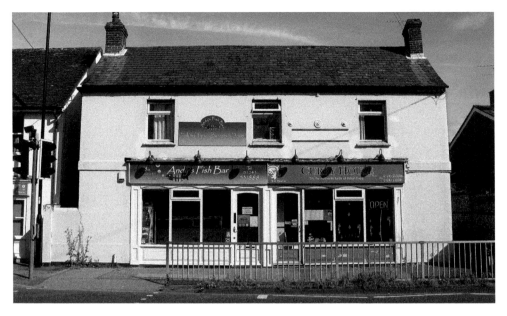

Red Lion.

60. Wheatsheaf, Nos 64–65 Oving Road (WG-T)

Together with No. 66, the two buildings that comprised the pub form an L-shaped trio. No. 64, red brick and prominent, appears to be of the late nineteenth century. In a semicircular plaque on the first floor of the grey-brick cottage of No. 65 appears the date 1816 above the inscription 'Will Ayling, Bricklayer', although the stone is now weathered and the details difficult to discern. The Wheatsheaf was in existence by 1871 under landlord Thomas Scarterfield, who also advertised as caterer to the Chichester Cattle Market. The pub was the headquarters of the Loyal 'Perseverance' Lodge of the Manchester Unity Independent Order of Oddfellows, which in July 1897 celebrated its 25th anniversary by a parade followed by a dinner here. The lodge was still meeting at the pub in 1909. Licensee from 1933–44, Thomas Jesse Eastland was Mayor of Chichester from 1947–49. His wife Alice, who held the licence from 1944–57, was Mayor in 1953–54. Both were made Honorary Freemen of the City in 1959. That nothing came of the early 1955 proposal by owners Henty & Constable to rebuild the pub (sixteen years before its Grade II listing) was because the Westgate Brewery was soon afterwards to enter into a process of liquidation. The Wheatsheaf eventually closed in early 1997 and three years later the site was converted into flats and houses. The developer placed a time capsule in the cellar before sealing it off. This contained a brick from the 1816 building with a thumbprint, presumably of Will Ayling, visible in the mortar, plus a bag of coins found in the pub and dating back to the early 1900s.

61. Barley Mow, No. 101 Oving Road (EA-F)

The use of these premises as a beerhouse dates back to the 1870s, and possibly earlier. From 1882–99 Charles Ide was both beer retailer and blacksmith here. The blacksmith side of

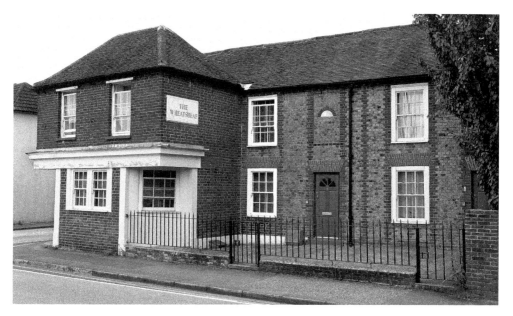

Above: Wheatsheaf.

Below: Wheatsheaf advert, *Moore's Chichester Directory 1880*.

72 CHICHESTER DIRECTORY, HANDBOOK AND ALMANAC, 1880.

WHEATSHEAF HOTEL, PORTFIELD

T. SCARTERFIELD,

Caterer to the Chichester Cattle Market.

——o——

WINES AND SPIRITS AT WHOLESALE PRICES.

the business was revived in the 1930s by Harry Dowling when Walter Rice was landlord. The pub closed in March 1998 after two years of complaints from residents and the police finally led to a refusal to renew its licence. It was converted to a private house by 2001.

62. Wickham Arms, No. 102 Bognor Road

This slate-roofed, flint-faced building was probably first licensed in 1861 when bricklayer Luke Janman had a beerhouse here or nearby in Bognor Road. For several years until 1871 it was known as the Jolly Waggoner under Thomas Spratt. The pub is on the corner

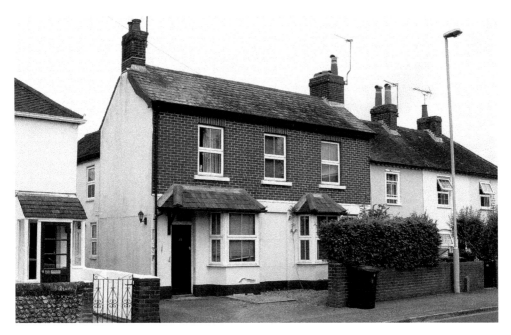

Above: Barley Mow.

Below: Wickham Arms.

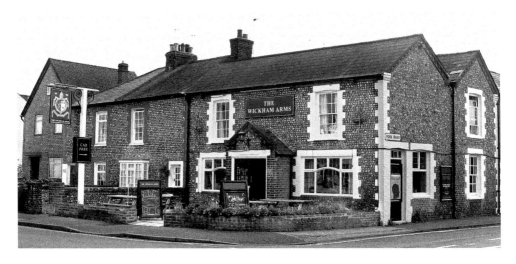

of York Road, previously Wickham Road, hence the source of the name change. It was owned from 1872 by a succession of small, local brewers until purchased in 1920 by lessee Gale's, who were themselves acquired in 2006 by current owners Fuller's.

63. Mainline Tavern, No. 35 Whyke Road

This was newly built and opened in May 1926 as the New Inn to replace an older house of the same name next door. The landlord at the time of the transition was

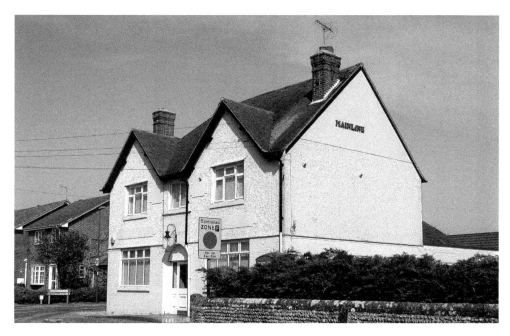

Mainline Tavern, formerly the New Inn.

Herbert Bere. Former Royal Marine John Boffin arrived here in 1971 with his wife Millie and their fifty-year-old parrot, Admiral Frobisher. The couple left in June 1989 and were the final tenants of Gale's. The inn was purchased by Chris Chapman (of Chapman's Inns, Worthing), who in 1990 organised a competition among the customers for a new name for the inn. The Mainline Tavern was chosen because the inn stands near the level crossing. It was closed by Greene King in 2008 and converted to residential use. The original New Inn existed by 1861 under James Smith who had come from the nearby Crown Inn. He was succeeded by his son George, who, like his father before him, was a ginger beer manufacturer.

64. Crown Inn, No. 140 Whyke Road (SS-WG-T)
An abstract of a will of 1762 makes reference to this property as 'now and for many years past bearing the sign of the Crown in Rumboldswhyke'. The pub retained the large part of its original thatched room until 1949. In 2014, it was sold by Greene King to become the Mexican restaurant, Muchos Nachos at the Crown. The locals regard the venue as a valuable social hub of the community and so were much relieved in spring 2017 when the present owners failed in their planning application to turn the Grade II-listed premises into housing.

65. Four Chesnuts, No. 234 Oving Road (EW-EA-F)
An article in the *Sussex County Magazine* of October 1936 remarked on the obscure origins of quaint inn names such as the Four Chestnuts. The November issue printed a reply from a reader who stated this particular name to be 'not a mystery' and related

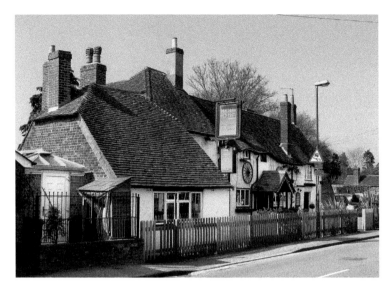

Crown Inn.

that that the inn was built around the 1860s or 1870s, being the property of noted city Councillor Edward Habin who traded nearby in horses. One of his customers was Sir Henry de Bathe who promised that if the inn was to be called the Four Chestnuts he would himself give the sign. This was duly done and 'on one side were four chestnut horses harnessed to a coach with Sir Henry handling the ribbons and a groom at each horse's head. On the reverse, the same team was shown going at a canter with Sir Henry driving'. The correspondence is, however, silent on another mystery of why the name was at first spelt Chesnuts instead of Chestnuts, a quirk revived in 1986 by licensees Jeff Glass and Carol Thackeray. The mystery of the missing 't' was the feature of a local newspaper article of 1998, in which licensee Andre Recknell JP was offering a champagne dinner for two to anyone with information on the matter.

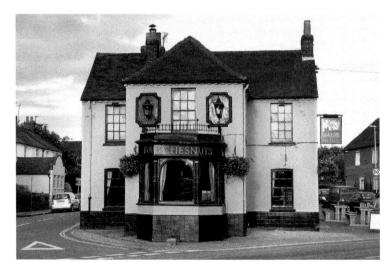

Four Chesnuts
(with missing 't').

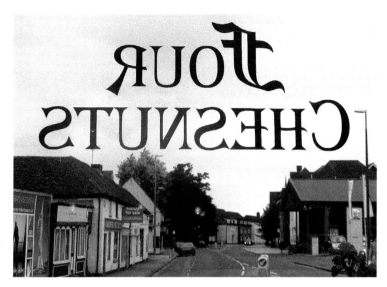

Through a window
(since replaced),
7 September 2008.

The time period given in the aforementioned reply also requires that Habin soon sold the pub, for it is first identifiable by name in an 1870 directory (with missing 't', so presumably not merely a signboard writer's error) under landlord George Wood and two years later is recorded as being in the ownership of Charles John Atkey of the East Walls Brewery. That the pub is a landmark feature of a major junction has led to its inclusion on the City of Chichester Local Buildings List. It is interesting therefore to consider that in 1946 this spot had been earmarked for road improvement. The city surveyor had that year been in negotiations with owning brewery Friary, Holroyd & Healy with a view to them selling the site for clearance and rebuilding the pub on part of the land known as Pound Farm Stables. No correspondence has been uncovered as to why the move did not take place. In 2007, the Four Chesnuts was voted Western Sussex CAMRA branch Pub of the Year under joint licensees Jamie Boyle, his mother Julia and her partner Peter Lowe. The pub reopened in spring 2017 following a six-month closure and extensive renovation.

66. Blacksmiths Arms, No. 110 The Hornet (C)
Now a fish and chip restaurant, this was a beerhouse by 1855 under licensee and blacksmith William Farley. The landlord from 1888–1904, Alf Tupper was also a registered sanitary plumber. After the licence renewal was refused in 1913, landlord John Sait traded here as a furniture dealer.

67. Castle, No. 21 The Hornet (KT)
This was a beerhouse by 1870. John Puttick, landlord from 1874–96, was also a painter, lath renderer and timber merchant. In 1915, Joe Grainger was convicted of assaulting landlord John Hawkes in Whyke Lane. Grainger owed Hawkes 5s but agreed to settle the debt only if Hawkes would collect it from Grainger's house. The men were walking there, Hawkes holding hands with his young daughter, when Grainger suddenly punched him in the face, causing Hawkes to fall to the ground

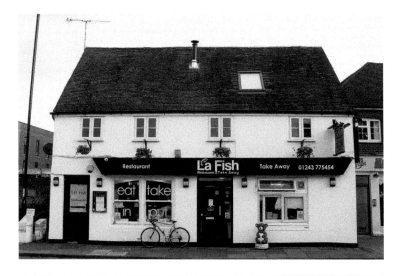

Blacksmiths Arms.

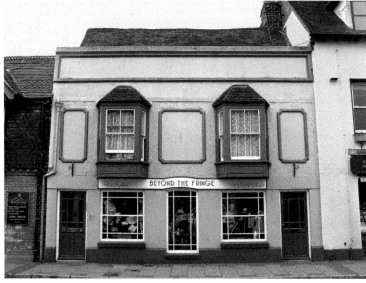

Castle.

and dragging his daughter down with him. Hawkes lost two teeth and his daughter sustained facial and bodily bruising. The following year John's wife Fanny was fined for selling beer outside permitted hours. The licence renewal was refused in 1921, after which Hawkes continued to occupy the premises for some years as a boot repairer.

68. Half Moon, No. 20 The Hornet (WG)

In 1730 this was called the Old Carbineer, subsequently the Half Moon. The landlady of July 1789 committed suicide by hanging herself from the staircase. The inn was listed as the Half Moon & Seven Stars in directories from 1804–51. Here in January 1837, a butcher and cattle dealer named Mr B. Green was presented with a silver tankard by a large group of local butchers and farmers 'to show their sense of peculiar

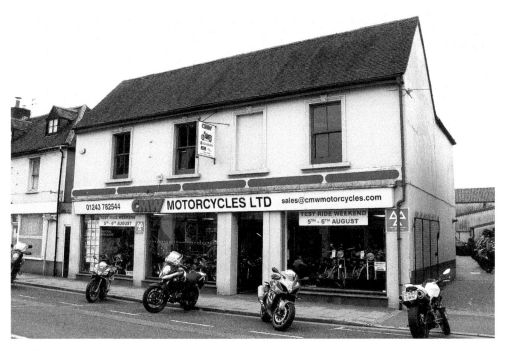

Half Moon (once with Seven Stars).

advantages they have long derived from their transactions with him at Chichester Market'. When the inn was sold at auction in 1848 it was mocked in the local press as a most ancient house much dilapidated, the lower floor often flooded and overrun by rats. Despite these insalubrities, it continued as an inn and lodging house until rebuilt in 1888 as larger premises also occupying the site of the former Black Horse pub and lodging house (known 1861–81 and not to be confused with the beershop of that name in St Pancras). The license renewal was refused in 1935 and the building became the British Legion Club before acquiring its current commercial use.

69. Bush, No. 16 The Hornet (EW-EA-F)
A sizable inn called the Dog & Duck was recorded on or near this site from 1670 to 1745. The more recent pub was known from 1858, first as the Prince Albert then from February 1896 as the Bush. In those days it was also a lodging house with a front shop. The change of name occurred with the arrival of landlady Eliza Clarke, who stayed for just eight months. If we discount her brief tenure then the inn was remarkable for having just three licensees in an eighty-seven-year period, but the first two of these – John Grist (1882–96) and James Veal (1896–1913) – were fly-by-nights compared to Fred North, who was landlord from September 1913 to July 1969 – from before the First World War to the first men on the moon. This was a Lambert & Norris house by 1889 and retained the sanded lettering advertising this Arundel brewery on both front windows until 11 January 1991, when one was broken by a customer aggrieved at being asked to leave due to drunkenness. The other was removed when the pub was converted to retail use after its closure in 2012.

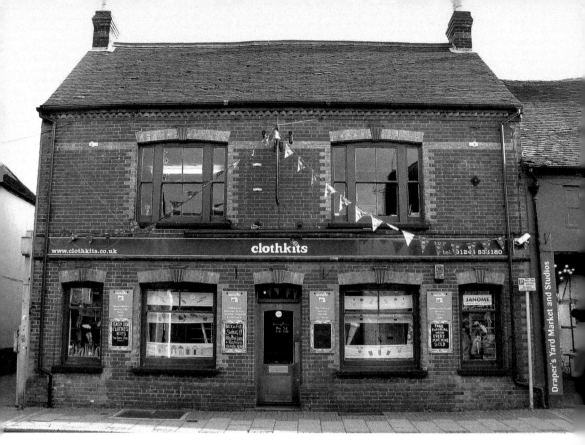

Bush, formerly Prince Albert.

The Landlords
Well-known local character John Grist (1845–1916) was landlord of the Cattle Market Inn in Eastgate Square from 1874–76 before arriving at the Prince Albert, adroitly combining the occupation of publican with that of fishmonger and grocer. He afterwards became a jobmaster (a man who hired horses and carriages for a specific task or period of time) operating from Richmond House, almost opposite his former pub.

70. Eastgate, No. 4 The Hornet

The sign depicts the East Gate of the city, above which was the gaol and gatehouse, demolished in 1783. The pub inhabits a Grade II-listed eighteenth-century building with a Victorian ground-floor frontage. By 1802 it was occupied by Stephen Wooldridge who had a brewhouse on site by 1811. Upon his death in 1849, his son Stephen Jr carried on the business. By 1861 it had been sold to brewer and wine and spirit merchant John Goldring. George Philips ran a grocery and beershop here in the late 1870s and was described as a 'practical brewer'. From the 1880s it was a public house only, yet continued as the Eastgate Brewery Inn until September 1952 when Gale's requested the deletion. Gale's had purchased the pub in 1929 but it was probably leased to them from 1879 by previous owners Martha Goldring (widow of John) and, from 1905, Maria Halstead (c. 1835–1927, wife of Charles Townsend Halsted of the

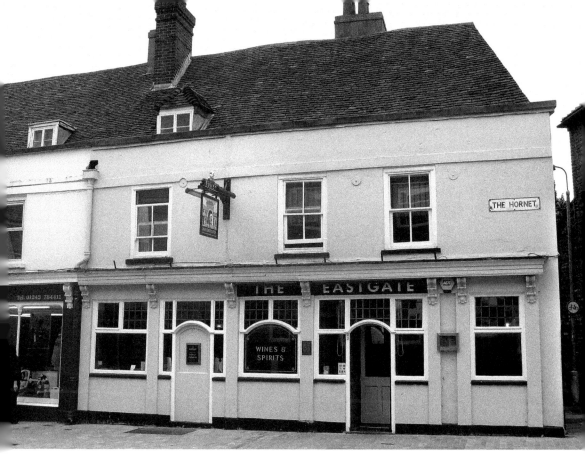

Eastgate, formerly Eastgate Brewery Inn.

local family of ironmongers, also a banker and twice Mayor of Chichester). During the late 1920s, under long-serving landlord James Montgomery Smith, the pub was a meeting place for the charitable organisation Ye Ancient Order of Froth Blowers.

In May 1962, Sir Laurence Olivier and his actress wife Joan Plowright treated landlord Fred Holder and his wife to drinks in the public bar in return for a kind deed. Mr Holder had helped out with supplies of bread and milk when the Minerva costumers of the Festival Theatre had moved into the former Unicorn over the road on a previous morning having first forgotten to notify the local bakers and dairy. The Eastgate was one of only three city pubs in the 1974 CAMRA *Good Beer Guide* – the first professionally published issue. The Bognor Regis & Chichester CAMRA branch was founded that year at a meeting in the back bar when George and Masie Barton were the hosts. In 1995, the interior with its front (public) and back (saloon) bars was remodelled into one room with the twitten entrance to the back bar put into disuse. In the days when the inn had three rooms, this side entrance led to a private bar. The landlady during the alterations, Angela Parsons, was the niece of former Beatle drummer Pete Best, who was unceremoniously sacked in favour of Ringo Starr. She displayed a signed photograph in the bar of her uncle from his time in the band. Gale's was acquired by Fuller's in 2006. Current co-licensee Catherine Allen is a recipient of their Master Cellarman Award.

Bibliography

Primary Sources
Pub History Society Library, newspaper articles on Chichester pubs
The Novium, Chichester Pubs Domesday Project
West Sussex Record Office
Add Ms, various
BO/CH/16/1, Building Plans
D1/3, Cutten Manuscripts
PS/CC/10, Petty Sessions Licensing Registers

Secondary Sources
Bishop, Rev'd John H., *A History of Summersdale, 2nd edition* (Chichester, 1984)
Brown, Edward, *Chichester in the 1950s* (Chichester: E. B. Publications, 1996)
Cutten, Mervyn James, 'Some Inns and Alehouses of Chichester', *The Chichester Papers*, 46 (Chichester: Chichester City Council, 1964)
Eddleston, John, J., *Chichester in the Great War* (Barnsley: Pen & Sword Military, 2016)
Green, Alan H. J., *The Building of Georgian Chichester, 1690–1830* (Chichester: Phillimore, 2007)
Green, Alan H. J., *The History of Chichester's Canal, 3rd edition* (Brighton: Sussex Industrial Archaeological Society, 2009)
Green, Alan H. J., 'The Ship Hotel, Chichester', *New Chichester Papers*, No. 6 (Chichester: Chichester Local History Society in association with The University of Chichester, 2014)
Green, Alan H. J., *Chichester in the 1960s* (Stroud: The History Press, 2015)
Holtham, Peter, 'The Brewers of West Sussex', *Sussex Industrial History*, No. 34, pp. 2–11 (2004)
Hudson, William Henry, *Nature in Downland* (London: Longmans, Green, 1900)
MacDougall, Philip, *Chichester Murders and Misdemeanours* (Stroud: Amberley, 2009)

McKenzie, Joyce, *Memories of Somerstown: A Tribute to a Community* (Wareham: Purbeck, 2008)

Morgan, Roy, *Chichester: A Documentary History* (Chichester: Phillimore, 1992)

Nairn, Ian and Pevsner, Nikolaus, *The Buildings of England, Sussex* (New Haven and London: Yale University Press, 2003)

Peart, Lester, 'The 1903 "Massacre" of City Pubs', *Chichester Observer*, Thursday 27 August 1987, p. 18

Pennington, Janet, 'The Inns and Taverns of Western Sussex 1550–1700: A Regional Study of Their Architectural and Social History', Unpublished PhD Thesis (University College Chichester, January 2003)

Saunders, Pat, 'Malting & Brewing in St Pancras, Chichester', *Brewery History*, No. 105, pp. 29–49, (Autumn 2001)

Saunders, Pat, 'Some Henty & Constable Houses', *Brewery History*, No. 106, pp. 25–37 (Winter 2001)

Saunders, Pat, 'Chichester Pubs: From the Barracks to the Railway Station', *Pub History: The Journal of the Pub History Society*, Issue 1, Vol. 1, pp. 16–18 (2002)

Saunders, Pat, 'Chichester Pubs West to East – From the Westgate Brewery to The Hornet and St Pancras', *Pub History: The Journal of the Pub History Society*, Issue 2, Vol. 1, pp. 7–12 (Spring 2003)

Smith, R. M. (ed.), *Alka-Seltzer Guide to the Pubs of Sussex* (London: Bayard Books, 1974)

Steer, Francis William, 'The Dolphin & Anchor Hotel, Chichester', *The Chichester Papers*, 23 (Chichester: Chichester City Council, 1961)

Thomas, Emlyn, *Georgian Chichester, Volume 1* (Middleton-on-Sea, 2000)

Trust Houses Ltd, *Tales of Old Inns, No. 53: The 'Dolphin & Anchor' at Chichester, in Sussex* (London: Trust Houses Ltd, 1936)

Walkerley, Rodney, L., *Sussex Pubs* (London: Batsford, 1966)

Willis, Thomas Gordon, *Records of Chichester* (Chichester: T. G. Willis & Co., 1928)

Journals and Magazines

Chichester History: The Journal of the Chichester Local History Society, all volumes, 1985–2017

Sussex Drinker: Magazine of the Sussex Branches of the Campaign for Real Ale, all issues, 1996–2017

Websites

Ancestry, http://www.ancestry.co.uk

Chichester District Council, https://publicaccess.chichester.gov.uk/online-applications

Find My Past, http://www.findmypast.co.uk

Acknowledgements

The author would like to thank the following for their help in facilitating the writing of this book: Amy Roberts, Collections Officer at the city museum, the Novium; Laurence Foord, Licensing Manager at Chichester District Council; all the very knowledgeable and helpful staff at the West Sussex Record Office and the local studies sections of the Chichester and Worthing public libraries; and to my employer, the University of Chichester, for reimbursement of the modest expenses incurred in the course of the research, which consisted mostly of short journeys to libraries and archives and leisurely early morning strolls to photograph the pubs while the streets were empty and quiet. All photographs that appear in this book were taken by the author.

The research endeavour was much eased by the groundwork laid in this area by the late Mervyn Cutten – JP, Archivist to the Corporation of St Pancras and landlord from 1964–2006 of the Murrell Arms at Barnham – and all those working on the Chichester Pubs Domesday Project of the mid-1980s, particularly Lester Peart, former chairman of the local branch of CAMRA. Lester continued to annotate the project papers with updates and then thoughtfully donated the collection to the Novium, where Amy kindly allowed this author to access it. This book is dedicated to both of these gentlemen in addition to all past and present licensees of the city's many hostelries over the centuries.